THE FIRST CENTURY

And Not Ready
For the Rocking Chair Yet

———————

Martha Ann Miller

Blessings
Martha Ann

The First Century: And Not Ready for the Rocking Chair Yet

Library of Congress Control Number: 2012917445

Miller, Martha Ann
The first century and not ready for the rocking chair yet /
By Martha Ann Miller — 1st ed.
1. Biography I. Title

ISBN 978-0-9882937-1-7 (Hardcover)

First Edition

Printed in USA

Cover photo by Mukti Desai, courtesy of AAUW
Cover and interior design by Rhonda Lee

Table of Contents

Foreword

Martha Ann Miller has been a mentor and friend to me for the last four years. How honored I have been to help bring her dynamic life story to book form! Imagine the documentary film we might have produced in the process: the laughing, crying, and praying; the arguing and reconciling; the bonding.

I consider Martha Ann to be family, and I am grateful for her presence in my life. Her farm-girl sensibilities, Midwestern accent, and no-nonsense, thrifty approach to living became an antidote for the sadness I felt after the loss of my maternal grandmother in 2008.

This remarkable woman has inspired my husband Bryan, who also helped to edit this book, and me by her desire to be used by God to do His work. She truly understands that nothing in this world is hers: Everything is God's. To see this example lived out in person has convinced me that when we live our lives to His glory, we are given all we need. Her story affirms this.

And, she has done something both courageous and necessary: put her life into print. How much richer this community, her family, and I are for the time, effort, and energy she has given to preserve these precious memories.

Martha Ann, happy 101st birthday! May God continue to use you and your story for years to come.

Joyfully,
Marci B. Schiller
Arlington, Virginia
August 2012

Acknowledgements

My heart is full of thanksgiving for the people who have helped me produce this book. Marci Schiller has been deeply involved, untangling the inevitable garbles that are produced by voice-recognition software. Later, she typed swiftly as I dictated scenes from my life, gently suggesting improvements. Her husband, Bryan Schiller, polished the prose. Both have been involved with the writing and editing of this book for four years.

None of this would have been possible without the computer expertise of Rod Swearingen, who guided my computer and software purchases, unfailingly stopping by to assist me any time I called on him. My grandson David Filiatrault provided expertise online and on the phone every time I got stuck.

J. Paul Lewis scanned most of the photographs used in this book and also took the pictures at the wonderful open house at Clarendon United Methodist Church for my 100th birthday. My son-in-law Philip Filiatrault photographed the church reception and also our intimate family group at the birthday dinner the evening before. Unless otherwise noted, all the photographs in this book are in my collection.

Latecomers to the process were my nephew, John Allen, and his wife, Jo, who assisted with rewriting, editing, proofreading and last-minute logistics. My daughter Margaret Filiatrault made several valuable suggestions that have enriched the book.

Rhonda Lee worked miracles with the photographs and designed the cover as well as the pages you're about to read.

Of course, this story could not have been told without all of the people who have been my eyes since 2005 when I became legally blind. Thanks to the many helpers who have made it possible for me to live on my own since then, I had the opportunity to write this autobiography.

While I have had lots of help with this little book, the errors you find in it are mine alone. I think I still have a pretty good memory, but I'm human, so I would like to hear about any corrections you may have.

Martha Ann Miller

Introduction

I never dreamed of writing a book until I found myself telling about events of the past that were exciting, full of history, and unique. How we handle major life events, and the decisions we make throughout our life, are what make us who we are. So now, after years of talking about writing the story of my life, I am finally serious about writing, particularly, since I don't have as many years left to accomplish this task.

Who will want to read my life's story remains to be seen. My precious family and friends have encouraged me, and I must not disappoint them. Therefore, I dedicate these memoirs to my daughter, Margaret Ann, who has been patient and loving, gently nudging me on; and to my son, Malcolm, who has always encouraged me to get started. I'd also like to dedicate these memoirs to my four grandchildren, David, Michael, and Annette Filiatrault (children of Meg and Phil), and Brian Payne, son of Winifred and Bob.

My family gathered for a portrait in the early 1990s. From left, son-in-law Bruce Kriebel, daughter Winifred Kriebel, grandson Brian Payne, me, grandsons Mike and David Filiatrault, daughter Meg Filiatrault, granddaughter Annette Filiatrault, son-in-law Phil Filiatrault and son Malcolm Miller.

To quickly summarize my life, I was born into a Christian family, have always tried to live a Christian life, to think of others and their needs, and to share what I have with others. This is the real joy of living for me. God has blessed me in so many ways that my life has been full of hope, faith, and love. I thank God for who and what I am today, and I look forward to what is yet to be.

Having lived most of my life in the 20th Century, it is worth noting what an incredible century it was. I've lived through the days of horses and buggies, trolley cars, Model-T Fords, and early airplanes. During my life, men have traveled to the moon and back. I can recall days as a young girl before electricity reached the farm, when our source of light at night was a coal-oil lamp that needed to be filled and cleaned each day. Then along came the Aladdin lamp, which was much brighter but required a mantel that had to be replaced often. The arrival of electricity was a blessing in many ways on the farm, and for society, it brought the Industrial Revolution.

I will cover all of these events, and many more, as I write the story of my life. So, as you read the story of my earlier years, imagine yourself living without a telephone, any electricity, running water, indoor bathroom, car, radio, television, computer, furnace, air conditioning, airplanes, tape—recorders, etc. Let me hasten to say that I have very fond memories of growing up on a farm in southern Indiana: breathing fresh air, making and eating homemade ice cream every Sunday during the summer months after getting home from church; and I am excited about recording the journey of my life through the nine decades of the 20th Century. I fully believe that there will never be another century as full of change and inventions as that one.

Martha Ann Miller

Chapter One

Preparing for the Journey

My ancestors came from large, working-class families. My maternal grandfather, who was German, was a butcher by trade, and my paternal great-grandfather, who was English, was a hotelier in Ireland. As immigrants, they arrived in America with little more than their determination and their faith. Since I have vivid memories of Grandmother Stahl and Grandfather Riggs, I became interested in their ancestors and why they came to America, and I want to pass that along to future generations. Here are some of the facts I have uncovered about them.

The Stahl Family History

Gottleb Stahl was born in January, 1834, in Lomersheim, Wuerttemberg, Germany. According to the family oral history, he came to America to escape mandatory training for military duty in the German army. He settled in German Township near Evansville, Indiana.

A generation earlier, another German family by the name of Laubscher had immigrated to America. They settled in German Township, near the German Methodist Church on Kratzville Road. They had a daughter, Barbara Susanna Laubscher, who was born February 4, 1840, and grew up in the community.

At the age of 22, Gottleb Stahl married Barbara Susanna Laubscher on May 29, 1856 in Kratzville, Indiana. They lived in a big brick house on Stringtown Road where they had a large family of six boys and six girls, one of whom was my mother, Minnie Rachel Stahl. Mother spoke of her father as being an educated man of strong character who followed his father's trade by becoming a butcher.

After Gottleb was married, he soon established a partnership with William Yokel in the butcher business. They lived near each other on Stringtown Road, and the butcher shop was a few miles down the road in Evansville.

My Grandmother Barbara Susanna Laubscher Stahl, seated left, with her youngest daughter, Gertrude Stahl Moore, standing; Great-grandmother Marie Swahlen Laubscher, seated, and my mother's oldest sister, Mary Stahl Ewing, seated right. Clothes were stored in the armoire, background, and the woven rag rug was handmade.

My mother, Minnie Stahl, seated, with a young friend.

The Riggs Family History

I knew that Grandfather Robert Riggs, at the age of nine, had emigrated with his family from Westmeath, Ireland, to the United States. I lived many years thinking that "Riggs" was an Irish name, but found out differently. On a trip to Ireland in 1997, we visited a man who had researched the Riggs family history. Apparently, some of the Riggs family in England had gone with Cromwell to Ireland to fight in a war in the 1640s, and decided to stay in Ireland. Later, in 1775, a descendant, Thomas Riggs, married a woman whose last name was Conner, and they had 16 children, six girls and 10 boys. Since the mother was Catholic and the father was Protestant, they decided to raise the girls Catholic, and the boys Protestant.

Research of the family history revealed that three girls stayed in Ireland and three moved to the United States and settled in New York City. One of the 10 boys, William Riggs (1797-1866), married Margaret Mossman (1805-1870) in about 1834 in Castle Pollard, where they lived. William, who was my great-grandfather, established a hotel business on the corner of the town square in County Westmeath, Ireland, about 35 miles northwest of Dublin and near Castle Pollard. They lived in the back part of the hotel, and they had seven children. My grandfather, Robert Riggs, was the third child.

About 1845, Ireland had a big potato famine. Many people were leaving Ireland, and the hotel business was suffering. William and Margaret Riggs decided to move their family to America.

To prepare for the trip, they packed all they could into a dray (a two-wheel cart) and started their journey to America. After reaching Dublin, they found passage to Liverpool. Here, they located a ship that was sailing for New Orleans. This was exactly where they wanted to go because other friends were already living there. Since there was room on the ship for the entire family, they boarded and set sail for America. This was a long trip of about nine weeks. During the voyage the youngest, a girl, took sick and died, and had to be buried at sea.

When they were almost to port, a storm developed and took them back out to sea; it was another week before they finally reached New Orleans. They were out of food by this time, and hungry. According to family lore, the captain threw a crust of bread to Margaret to keep her youngest child from crying.

This was not an easy trip for them to make, but they finally arrived at the port of New Orleans on December 21, 1847. Grandfather Riggs said that his father, my great-grandfather Riggs, had $1.75 in his pocket when they docked. Their friends, who had emigrated earlier, took them into their homes. The family stayed in New Orleans for the rest of the winter.

In the spring of 1848, they traveled up the Mississippi River to St. Louis by boat. After staying in St. Louis for two summers, they continued up the Ohio River to Evansville, Indiana. At first they settled in German Township, and later moved to a farm in the Bluegrass community. Robert's youngest brother, John, fought in the Civil War, and was killed in Kentucky on October 8, 1862, in the Battle of Perryville.

Two other brothers moved to Princeton, Indiana, 40 miles north of Evansville, to settle.

Tom was Grandfather Robert Riggs' oldest brother. In 1860, when Tom was 25 years old, he married Ann Smith, who was 19. Several months later it started to rain as he was helping to roof a barn. He told Robert to get in out of the rain, but Tom kept working. Following this exposure, he caught pneumonia and died. Before his death he asked Robert to marry his wife, which Robert did. Robert and Ann had a large family of 12 children, six boys and six girls; three of the girls died young. Most of the other children grew up, married, and settled within the Bluegrass community or in nearby Kratzville or McCutchanville.

Robert and Ann Riggs.

The family of Robert and Ann Riggs.

My Immediate Family History

My parents were Minnie Rachel Stahl, born June 4, 1875, the ninth child of Gottleb and Barbara Stahl, and William Robert Riggs, born September 16, 1867, the third child of Robert and Ann Riggs.

I never asked my parents how they met, but they were married September 27, 1893. Mother was 18 years old and Dad was 27. She wore a tan velvet dress trimmed in dark red velvet with handmade lace on her petticoats; he wore a dark suit.

William Robert Riggs and Minnie Rachel Stahl Riggs in their wedding outfits.

My parents started their married life with very few material possessions: some personal belongings, a small bank account, a wagon, and a team of horses. Their first home was in a small old house off of Kratzville Road on 27 acres of land. While living here, they had two boys, Ralph and Arthur. Mother and Dad decided to build a bigger house.

To get the lumber for building, they cut down trees and carved beams, logs, and planks out of the wood. You can imagine how much work it was to build the new house.

They really wanted to own a larger farm, so when the railroad company came to them and asked to buy the 27 acres of land, they were happy to sell. They looked for a larger place and found a 125-acre farm near McCutchanville. Sometime after they moved, they heard that the house they had built was on fire! It is interesting to note that the hardwood trees they had used to build the house were the reason the frame stood, burning until it collapsed into a heap of hot coals. Mother and Dad started life on the larger farm with Ralph, 12, and Arthur, 8. After a few years Oscar was born, and four years later, I was born.

I know nothing about the first few years of my life, except that I slept in the bedroom with my parents and was in their loving care.

Now, I will write the exciting story of my life, by starting with a quick description of the layout of my family's farm.

The farm was in the shape of a rectangle. The house and barn and other buildings were located on the west end. Petersburg Road was in front of the house and ran diagonally across the northwest corner of the rectangle. On the north side was a fence dividing our farm from our neighbor's farm. This property line went quite a ways back to a railroad track that formed the east end of the farm. Along the south side was a public road that passed the end of the farm. A short fence between the two roads showed where the farm ended on the west side.

This was home the first 23 years of my life.

Our family farm.

Chapter Two

Babyhood to Second Grade

I put in my earthly appearance at about eight o'clock Sunday morning, August 6, 1911. The doctor arrived at our house by horse and buggy. He saw my three older brothers and told them to get lost and not to return until his horse and buggy were gone. When they ventured back, they found that they had a baby sister; I was now the youngest of four children.

My dad told me many years later how much I was really wanted. He said, "When you were born I went around telling everyone: 'I have a little G, a little I, a little R, a little L; I've got a little girl.'" Well, you know what? He told me this when I was home from college one summer, and ever since it has made me chuckle inside when I think about it and realize how much I really was wanted.

Martha Ann Riggs, about one year old.

The farm on which I was born and raised had a house, a barn, and a granary, where we stored harvested grain. As the farm work progressed, my parents had need of other buildings, such as a chicken house, a tool shed, and finally a new barn for the herd of cows, which was continually growing in number.

The house was a two-story building with a parlor and a small porch (beside the parlor) across the front. From the front porch we entered the living room, which was on the south side of the house. Next to the living room, on the north side, was Mother and Dad's bedroom. From the living room we entered a large dining/kitchen area, which had a north porch and a south porch. This gave the family good cross-ventilation when it was needed. This was where we cooked and ate in the winter. Twice a year, the dining/kitchen area changed. In the summer, we moved the wood/coal cook stove to a room on the back of the house where the laundry was done. This activity was moved out to the back yard (more about this later). The "summer" kitchen now provided more space to do canning and cooking during the warmer months.

The pantry—part of the dining room—was a fairly sizable storage space where the dishes were kept on shelves. The other side had shelves where the cooking supplies were kept, above the flour and sugar bins. My parents would buy 100 pounds of sugar and 100 pounds of flour at a time. These staples came in burlap bags lined with tightly woven cotton bags. When the cotton bags were empty, they would rip them open and make excellent towels for drying dishes. If the supply of this material got plentiful, we would make other items from it, such as curtains or aprons to use or sell.

We did the laundry outside under a shade tree. Since we didn't have running water, we used soft water from the cistern, which was filled with rainwater from the roofs of the buildings. We would pull up buckets full of water to fill the laundry tubs. Or, if we knew that it was about to rain, we would set the laundry tubs out in the yard to get a supply of clean soft water. Each of these tubs could hold at least 10 gallons of water; it took two of us to carry one. The tubs had handles opposite each other. We would heat some of the wash water on the stove in a copper boiler, which was large enough to fit over two burners. It was rounded at the ends (more on this later).

We could go upstairs either from the bedroom or the dining room. In the corner of the dining room was a set of steps that led up to a platform. There were also steps coming up from the bedroom to the same platform. Then, we turned and took more steps up to the hallway and the bedrooms.

Arthur and Oscar slept in the south bedroom, and my bedroom was at the front of the house. I had been told not to peek in as I went by their room. The third room was used as a storage room. Over the dining room was the attic where we kept up to 300 empty jars that were saved for our canning projects in the summer. All summer we would can the food that was needed to carry us through the winter months. The canned meat, vegetables, and fruits were stored in the cellar, which was located under the summer kitchen. To get to the cellar, we had to raise a trap door that was located along the south side of the summer kitchen. When we raised the trap door, leaning it against the wall, there were steps leading down to a dirt floor. On a few occasions, some water would get on the floor and it would take time for it to dry out. But, when this happened, we would lay down wooden planks to walk on to get the food we needed. The cellar was usually a cool, dry place for storing our canned food. Since it was underground and under the summer kitchen, we never really worried about anything getting frozen. In very cold weather, we would hang a lighted lantern from the ceiling rafters in order to give off enough heat to keep the canned food from freezing.

South of the white-frame house was a big garden space that had three long rows of grape vines. Along the back yard and the garden was a dirt lane that led to the fields south of the house. Around the house was a green lawn with flowers, bushes, and red brick walks. North of the house was a nice-sized triangular area called the barnyard. This space was enclosed by a fence between the house and the barnyard, a hedge that included trees along the road, and a fence from the road along the north side of the horse barn. This yard had a gate that opened in from the road. A short fence and another gate were enough to keep the horses in the yard. In this yard were the cistern and a deep well (the source of all our drinking water), which took care of our water needs.

On top of the well was a strong wooden platform that held a pump and a trap door large enough to put a bucket through. Since we did not have an icebox, we would put butter and other food that needed to be kept cool into a bucket, and lower it down into the well with a rope. To get water to drink, the pump had to be primed. We always kept a bucket full of water hanging on the pump, along with a dipper. To prime the pump you would pour water into the top of the pump and start pumping at the same time. The water would then start coming up and go into a watering trough for animals to drink. As we pumped, we would fill several buckets with water for use in the kitchen. Every so often, Dad would test the water to see if it was healthy to drink. Our well was considered to be very good: It was deep enough and located near an underground source. I do not remember it ever going dry, and this was fortunate, as some farmers had to haul water during very long dry spells.

After a day's work, the men working on the farm would unharness the horses and draw water by the buckets full to pour into the cistern watering trough. Then Dad would let the horses relax and run around the yard or go into the barn to eat hay for their supper. For our family, the day was not yet over.

Mother was putting the finishing touches on dinner. It was usually my job to set the table and help get the food on the table. Once everything was ready, we would gather around the table, sit down, and Dad would lead us in prayer. Dinnertime was a time to enjoy a wonderful meal and one another's company. After a short time of rest, the men would go out to the new barn and get the cows ready to milk while Mother and I washed the dishes and tidied up the kitchen. I could hardly wait to run out to the barn to help milk the cows, which numbered 12 to 15. Mother would often join us. When we finished milking it would be nearly 9 p.m. and time for me to go to bed.

Petersburg Road, in front of our farm, continued up the road in a northeasterly direction, crossed the Hornby farm, went up a steep hill, and out into the country. This road went past the school building and church area in McCutchanville, Indiana.

From Petersburg Road, there was a fence (on the property line) that led to the railroad tracks at the back of the farm. On our side of the fence was a lane leading to the fields on the right side of the lane and to a six-acre field that was north of the woods. Here was a gate. This field and the woods were fenced in so the cows could be put out to pasture without being watched. In the woods was a pond that had water for the cows to drink, shade trees to rest under, and grass in the field for them to eat. With proper care, the cows would produce more milk, which was our cash income every month.

To get to the back "forty," we cut diagonally across the pasture to the corner of the woods where we opened a gate to reach the acres at the back of the farm. Since Dad rotated the crops, this large field was where we raised corn, wheat, hay, and whatever we needed to feed the animals. Any surplus was considered our "cash crop" and was usually sold to pay the taxes and other farming expenses. There was a nice big orchard east of the house where we had all kinds of fruit trees. A lot of our time was spent canning fruit all summer as the different fruits became ripe. We also raised pigs, chickens, and sometimes ducks.

Dad and Mother were always considered good farmers, and they took pride in their work. I am so grateful for having been born into this loving Christian family that held me to a high standard of living by teaching me how to work, save, and to be honest and truthful.

My brother Ralph always called me "Sis." Since he was 15 years old when I was born, he was not a part of the household for very much longer, being married when he was 20. One of my vivid memories of childhood was holding their infant son in my arms. Little Leroy was the first of Mother and Dad's 15 grandchildren and my first nephew!

Another memory is of Grandmother Stahl, who would stay with us every summer for several weeks at a time. She slept in our parlor, where we had a pull-down bed that looked like a chest when it was not in use. She would often sit on a low rocking chair by the north screen door in the summer kitchen to sew while Mother was busy cooking or canning.

One day when I was three years old, she started to sit down on the rocking chair, but missed the chair and fell on the floor. Mother called me to come and said, "Run! Get Dad! Tell him to come! Grandma has fallen!" Dad was working in the garden, south of the house. Around this time I was just beginning to talk so I remember running, grabbing his hand and pulling him toward the house, trying to tell him something. It turned out that Grandma had broken her hip, and Dad helped Mother to take care of her. I don't remember much of what happened after that, but Grandma Stahl died on October 27, 1914, a few weeks after her fall.

I spent a lot of time with Mother during my pre-school days. My brothers were usually out in the field working with Dad. There was always lots of work to do on the farm. There were many cherished times when Dad would take me along with him if he were going to pick up seeds to be planted or on other errands where I would not be in the way.

One of my earliest memories is of sleeping on a cot in Mother and Dad's bedroom. Instead of pulling up the covers when I was cold, I'd hop out of bed, and go over and crawl in between Mother and Dad, where it was nice and warm. Then I would lie as still as possible, and they went back to sleep. There were other times when I'd wake up and be so scared that I wouldn't move a muscle because I had dreamt there was a big snake outside my window. When I was fully awake, I knew it was a dream and went back to sleep.

My dad, William Robert Riggs.

Dad was always the first one up in the morning. He would shake down the ashes in the living room stove and add wood from the wood box in the corner. When the wood started to burn, he would add more wood and coal. In time, there would be a nice fire burning, and the boys were called to get dressed by the stove. I got to sleep a little longer; then it was my turn to get dressed. By that time, the living room was nice and warm. After I was dressed, I would often run to the barn to play with the kitties. During these younger years, it was my job to go to the house to let Mother know how soon the men folk would be in for breakfast.

As I got a little older, my life began to change. I began sleeping upstairs, and the front bedroom was to be my bedroom—all by myself. Since it was over the parlor, no one could really hear me if I got up and walked around. Usually, I was so tired I'd crawl in bed and be fast asleep in no time.

My parents had box springs and a mattress on their bed, but mine was a straw mattress in summer and a feather mattress in winter for warmth. I particularly liked summer, when we had fresh straw from the wheat harvest. We'd empty the ticking, wash it,and stuff it with new straw. After the wheat was harvested and threshed, we had a big, fresh straw stack located between the horse barn and the cow barn. It was used to bed-down the animals for the rest of the year. The straw stack was about two stories high, but it would settle down when it rained.

After I slept in the bed for several nights and snuggled on the newly filled mattress, it soon became very comfortable. The straw would mash down, and I loved the aroma of the fresh straw. The bed was a double walnut bed, so there was plenty of room to move around; I felt so grown up to think I had a room all to myself. Of course, the room was not heated because we had no central heat, which was fine during the spring, summer, and fall, but oh, did it get cold in the winter! Whenever I got up in the morning, I'd wrap up and dash downstairs to dress by the stove.

When it got time to go to bed, Mother and I would take our regular walk to what we called the "outhouse" or privy since we had no bathrooms in the house. I might say here, that there was no toilet paper in those days, so we used the thin paper sheets in the Sears Roebuck catalogues. Or, we might have used these instead of buying toilet paper in order to save money. I don't remember what we used at school, but I know that the school buildings did not have running water either. Anyway, this was the type of country living. There was a water system for the people living in the cities; richer folks must have had toilet paper. When we got back in the house from our walk, I would get ready for bed. Then Mother would pick up a lamp and go upstairs with me. We would have prayer time together. We usually said,

"Now I lay me down to sleep.
I pray the Lord my soul to keep.
If I should die before I wake,
I pray the Lord my soul to take."

Then, she tucked me in and kissed me goodnight. She checked to see if the white china pot with a handle and lid was conveniently placed by my bed, in case I needed it during the night. I would only use it if I absolutely had to because every morning it would have to be emptied, washed, and cleaned, which was a chore.

As I got older, I remember having a couple of friends over to stay all night, and we'd all try sleeping in the double bed. Since the straw mattress was not even, we'd tend to roll toward each other. Well, this was all fun, even if we didn't get much sleep; we were ready to sleep in our own beds the following night. These friends were Alice George and Bernice Bruner, who are still friends as I write this book. We all went to the same church, school, and lived near McCutchanville less than two miles from each other.

Every Sunday morning, our family would wake up and spend the morning getting ready to go to Sunday school and church. First, the cows had to be milked and fed. Chickens, horses, and other farm animals were fed. Then, a chicken needed to be killed and dressed, so that it would be ready to cook when we got home from church.

I will briefly describe the process of killing and dressing a chicken. The following may sound cruel, but it happened so fast that the chicken didn't know what happened to it. We had a large round block of wood on the ground in the backyard. A horseshoe was nailed to the side of the block of wood. First we caught a chicken by the leg with a wire hook on the end of a long pole. The chicken was held by the legs, laid on top of the block of wood, and the horseshoe was fitted over the chicken's head. With a sharp corn knife, we'd chop the chicken's head off.

After a few minutes the body of the chicken was dipped into a bucket of hot scalding water. This would loosen the feathers from the skin so that we could pick them off; we saved the soft down feathers. Down feathers are the ones on the breast and legs of chickens and ducks. Whenever we killed a chicken to eat, we would save these soft feathers, wash and dry them, and store them to stuff our mattresses in the winter.

In the meantime, the cans of milk were set out on the side of the road for the milk truck to pick up. The milk was taken to the milk plant, processed, and delivered to the city folks. In the warmer months, we would keep an extra gallon and a half of milk out for making ice cream after church. When we ordered it, the milk truck driver would bring us 50 to 100 pounds of ice, which only cost 25 to 50 cents, for making ice cream. (The ice was wrapped in paper and burlap and stored in a laundry tub to keep it from melting too much before we got home.) This was our special Sunday treat, and was it delicious!

McCutchanville Methodist Church.

When we were all ready to leave for church, Dad would have the horse hitched up to the surrey (with a fringe on top). We would arrive at church about 9:20 a.m., around the same time as the other families in the neighborhood. Our church was a beautiful, small red-brick building situated on top of a hill. Inside was a nice-sized sanctuary with stained-glass windows. Across the back of the sanctuary were brown folding doors that could be closed, forming three small classrooms for the mixed-age children's Sunday school class. The adults met in different parts of the sanctuary.

Here is a brief history about the little red brick church on the hill: In 1842, the "seeds were sown" that grew and developed into the little red brick church on the hill that I remember.

In the beginning, a Methodist circuit rider was asked to come and hold meetings in the area, where a simple structure was built for $300 in this rural wilderness. The land was donated by Mr. and Mrs. Samuel McCutchan. It's amazing to think that this beautiful church was built by the men of the community during the busy planting and harvesting time and that it was free of debt when it was dedicated on November 28, 1880! The name, McCutchanville Methodist Church, demonstrated how highly regarded that family was in the community.

Our Sunday school teachers gave us many things to memorize, such as the Lord's Prayer and the 23rd Psalm. At another time we had to find a verse in the Bible that started with each letter of the alphabet. For example: "Do unto others as you would have others do unto you" (Luke 6:31); "Honor thy father and thy mother" (Ex 20:12); "I was glad when they said to me 'Let us go into the house of the Lord.' " (Ps 122:1). After the Sunday school class selected the best verses that it found for each letter, we would memorize those verses. We also memorized a number of songs that I still love to sing.

There was one song in particular that I liked: "We've a Story to Tell to the Nations." Here are the words to the first stanza:

"We've a story to tell to the nations,
That shall turn their hearts to the right,
A story of truth and mercy,
A story of peace and light,
For the darkness shall turn to dawning,
And the dawning to noonday bright,
And Christ's great kingdom shall come on earth,
The kingdom of love and light."

After the church service, we would often visit with the other families for awhile and then head for home. Mother would start cooking dinner while the rest of the family was making the ice cream or setting the dinner table.

To make the ice cream, we had a wooden ice cream bucket with a tall metal can that fit inside the wooden bucket with a hand crank attached to the top of it. We'd all take turns turning the crank to stir the milk inside the can. The ice was cracked by putting large chunks of ice from the ice block into a burlap sack and hitting it with an ax. The cracked ice and salt were put around the can inside the wooden bucket and in due time the milk froze and was ready for packing. To pack the ice cream, the salt water would be poured off through a hole on the side of the wooden bucket. Then more ice and salt were added to keep the ice cream frozen until ready to eat. The salty ice water was saved and used to pour over the red-brick walkway where the grass was growing. The salty water would kill the grass and help keep the walkway pretty and red.

During my pre-school days, I really did not have many children to play with. Oscar, my youngest brother, was about four years older, and we had fun times together, but it was nothing like having someone to play with all the time. He had a red wagon that I could sit in, and he would pull me around the yard. Sometimes he would go much faster than I liked, and Mother would make him stop. Our nearest neighbor was the Hornby family. They had four girls and one boy. Madge was my age, and sometimes Mother would let me go to their house to play, but both families were so busy during the week that I spent most of my time with Mother. She was always very patient with me and started teaching me how to be helpful at a very early age. In the fall of the year, when Oscar started back to school, I asked Mother when it would be my time to go to school and she said, "You will be old enough in one more year." I thought that year would never pass because I was so anxious to get started.

At a very early age, I loved to climb ladders. Dad had the ladder set up to pick cherries. The cherries were ripe, the tree was large, and I wanted to climb the ladder and pick cherries.

Dad taught me how to hold on to the ladder so I wouldn't fall. He even let me climb very high and took my picture in the cherry tree.

Dad would spray the fruit trees every spring so the fruit would be free of worms when it was ready to pick. This was especially important for the cherry trees; otherwise we would have to open each cherry by hand to check for worms. Dad, however, always seemed to know when to spray, and we could use the cherry seeder instead. This was really a neat gadget that made seeding cherries much faster than doing it by hand. The seeder had two curved prongs that went over the cherries and pushed the seeds through two small holes in the bottom of the tray holding the cherries. When the prongs were swung up from the tray, the seeded cherries would drop and roll down into a pan that we held on our laps.

We would heat quart jars in the oven to sterilize them. Then we cooked the cherries, put them into the jars, screwed the lids on tight, and put the jars in boiling hot water. We left the cherry-filled jars in the boiling water for 20 to 30 minutes. This last step was to be sure the jars were completely sealed and would keep all winter. One year, Mother and I canned 100 quarts of cherries! We were able to make cherry pies all through the winter.

Another fruit that we loved to can in large amounts was the Maiden Blush apple. These apples were the first to ripen and made wonderful applesauce. Sometimes, we would peel and slice the apples and cook them in water. This way, the slices would stay whole, and we would can the slices with the juice. During the winter, we would put the sliced apples onto a piece of bread and add milk. With a little cinnamon on the top, this was an easy Sunday evening dessert that was almost as good as apple cobbler. We would eat leftovers and a simple dessert like this on Sunday evening, which was Mother's night off from cooking.

Dad always had a big garden with lots of produce. His two specialties were strawberries and asparagus. Strawberries were planted every year. Dad would make a ridge of dirt and put the strawberry plants into the ground on top of the ridge. Straw from the straw-stack was spread over the ground be-

23

tween the rows and up around the plants. The runners would grow on top of the straw and take root and grow another plant. The straw held the moisture in the ground and protected the strawberries from getting dirty when they ripened.

The nice thing about asparagus was that it came up each year from the roots in the ground. We just had to see that the soil was rich and weeds were not growing. We usually had all that we could eat and gave some away to family, neighbors, and friends.

Oh! I must tell you about the big swing we had on the side of our front yard. There were two tall poplar trees that stood about 10 to 12 feet apart. Dad and the boys put a pole through the branches of both trees and fastened it to the tree trunks. Then a strong rope was used to make the swing. The seat was long enough for one person, or two small people, and was strong enough to hold anyone in the family. Oscar and other family members would push me while I was on the swing. Sometimes Oscar would run under me to push me as high as he could—this was really fun. I could also pump and make the swing go high. Then I could sit down and just swing back and forth until the swing gradually stopped.

Near the swing was a fence covered with honeysuckle. When the plant was in bloom, it was especially fun to swing back and forth and smell the sweet scent of honeysuckle. I liked to pick the blooms of these plants. Sweet nectar was inside the blossoms, and I could pull out the stem and get a taste of it. I always checked to be sure a bee was not in the blossom.

The job of a honeybee was to collect nectar and pollen from the many different blossoms. The bee would return to the hive to store the nectar and convert it into honey in the combs for future use: for the bees to live on during the winter, or for people to eat. If you buy a jar of honey in the store, you should know that somewhere, a hive of bees worked hard to produce it. In the early days, many farmers kept several bee-hives near the orchard because the bees would pollinate the blossoms. As the bees flew from blossom to blossom, the pollen collected on their feet and would get brushed off onto the next blossoms that they landed on. All of this was necessary for fruit to develop on the tree from the flower. Isn't God's plan wonderful?

I never did have many toys to play with, but I especially liked two dolls and one piece of my grandmother's doll furniture, which I still have. My mother always liked to sew, and she would make something for my doll if she had some scraps left from another item she was making. Since we did not have electricity, she ran the sewing machine by pumping her feet up and down on a floor pedal that was connected with a belt to the sewing machine's head. I always wanted to be helpful and do everything that Mother was doing, but at the time I wasn't tall enough to operate the sewing machine properly. My method of learning to sew was the old- fashioned way involving a needle, thread, and thimble.

One day, I heard Dad say that it was time to start mowing hay. The next day, I was out in the barn and got the idea that I could help Dad by moving the grindstone away from the wall, which he usually did when he wanted to sharpen the mower machine blades before he started to mow hay. The grindstone was about 16 inches across and was mounted on a frame that looked very much like a tricycle without wheels and seemed big enough for an adult to sit on. The round stone was mounted vertically on the frame with foot pedals. One could push the pedals and make the stone go round and round. In trying to move this stone, I accidentally tipped it over, but fortunately, it did not break. My father scolded me for doing this and told me never to do it again.

He placed the grindstone over the cow manure trough because he always used water when he was sharpening the mowing machine blades. The water ran down into the trough so that the concrete floor could stay dry. The next day was a nice sunny day, so he was able to take the mowing machine into the field and cut the hay. I'll explain the harvesting of the hay later.

Another pastime of mine was catching fireflies, also known as lightning bugs. These were a type of beetle that would stay near the ground and in the grass during the day.

At dusk, these particular beetles would fly around about three feet from the ground.

As they lifted their wings to fly, a chemical reaction on each side of their abdomens would light up to attract a mate. To see thousands of these bugs flying over the fields, twinkling, was a beautiful scene. We could run all around the front yard catching them by hand and putting them into a glass jar with a hole in the lid. As it got dark, we would let the fireflies fly free.

In the early 1900s we still didn't have electric lights in our house, or a telephone. These two conveniences made the 20th century an incredible time in which to live. Can you imagine what it would be like, today, to live without a telephone or electricity?

The telephone, at that time in history, was the world's greatest invention for personal communication. It was invented by Alexander Graham Bell, who was a schoolteacher who came to the United States in 1871. He taught the deaf and started to do experiments to help people hear. The exciting story of how the telephone developed is recorded in history. But the first words heard over the telephone were in 1876. Much development took place before it became widely available to the communities throughout this country. During the first 15 years of the 20th century, many telephones were being installed throughout the United States.

During the 19th century, many immigrants were moving to the United States from different countries and for many reasons. Many of the immigrants were very intelligent people who wanted to have more freedom of religion and be able to do the things that they really wanted to do. Both the inventor of the telephone and the conjurer of electricity were born in the same year: 1847. Alexander Graham Bell invented the telephone, and Thomas Edison perfected several uses for electricity most notably, the light bulb. These men or their parents were immigrants. Much of the development of their achievements took place in this country. Most of their work was done in the 19th century, but their contributions made the 20th century an incredible time in which to live. In my humble opinion, the telephone and electricity were probably the two greatest advancements in the world.

Before I started school, we received our first telephone; when I was 10, we had electricity. Up until that time, these phenomena hadn't reached all the rural areas of Southern Indiana, so we had to wait until lines were installed along our roads before we could apply for the telephone and electric services. I remember the day when the serviceman arrived at our house to install our telephone on the wall in our living room. One had to stand up in front of the phone to answer it; I had to stand on a stool to reach it!

There were seven parties on one line, and we each had a different signal so we knew when a call was for us. Our signal was a short-short-long ring. We also knew each other's signals so if we wanted to talk with someone on our line, we could ring their signal without going through the telephone switchboard. When we wanted to talk to a neighbor on that same line, we had to crank the bell. The handle was on the right hand side on top. All other calls had to go through the telephone switchboard operator, who was located in a house near our church. The telephone company soon realized that its system was going to work only if the operator was good at the job. The operator would pull up two lines with plugs on the end and plug them into the switchboard. This was sometimes done at a very fast pace for multiple lines.

I read somewhere that the company only hired men to operate the switchboards, and instead of connecting the lines, they wanted to talk to people! When the company started hiring women, it was discovered that women did a much better job of operating the switchboards. This was considered a prestigious job for a woman in those early days, and I will also say that she usually knew what was going on in the neighborhood!

A good operator knew when to keep her mouth shut, and when it was okay to share any news that the community should know, such as a death in the neighborhood. In addition to the operator, anyone on our line could listen in on other people's conversations. Eavesdropping on someone's conversation was as easy as picking up the receiver: We never told any secrets over the telephone. One naughty thing that I loved to do was to very carefully remove the receiver from the telephone and very quietly listen to what other people were saying. Sometimes the people would stop talking and say, "Whoever is listening on the phone, would they please hang up." So I would hang up the receiver and leave the telephone alone until the next time I was tempted. It was fun standing on the stool listening in on conversations whenever Mother didn't know what I was doing.

I was about 10 years old when electricity service was available in our neighborhood. The Electric Light Company had to install tall poles along the road and attach the electricity line, up high, on the poles. Dad requested service as soon as it was available. None of the houses was wired for electricity, so this was a major project. Even though the electricity was brought into our lives, it did not mean that it was for the whole house: we started with only a bulb in the living room and one in the barn. The lines had to be insulated from the framework of the wooden house to prevent a fire from starting.

I do not remember how long it took to get full service, but that did come in time. Before then, I had used an Aladdin lamp to study by on the dining room table. And, we had our oil lamps to get around the house and the barn. It really was a big help to finally have electricity.

Before telling about my grade school days, I want to comment briefly about what was going on in the world at that time, and what other members of my family were doing.

The European countries were fighting each other in 1914, and the United States was supplying some of them with food and provisions that they needed. Other countries didn't like this and destroyed an American ship. On April 6, 1917, the United States declared war on Germany. In May, Congress passed a law stating that all single men between the ages of 18 and 31 would be drafted.

Since my oldest brother, Ralph, had been married in December, 1916, at the age of 20, this law did not affect him. Arthur had just turned 18 years old in March and so was eligible to be drafted.

It took the United States a fair amount of time to get our country ready to fight and get men drafted and trained. I remember listening to much discussion around the dinner table as to when Arthur might have to go, and how it would change things in our family. He had just graduated from high school and was planning on attending Evansville College. He started his studies that fall, and also began to sell Bibles so that he could earn money to go on to Purdue to get a degree.

As I remember it, Arthur had no desire of being a part of the fighting that was going on almost halfway around the world. He went into the Army when he was called in 1918. The family was relieved when the fighting stopped with an armistice on November 11, 1918, and the men could start coming home. I do remember that when Arthur got home, he took off his uniform, put it in the north storeroom and never mentioned his time overseas. The clothes hung there for a number of years. Mother and I would clean up the room every so often and leave them hanging on the rack.

On Memorial Day, about 1920, veterans of the Civil War, Spanish-American War and World War I gathered in the McCutchanville cemetery. Left to right: Charles H. McCutchan, Allan Patterson, Jacob Kreger, Roy Moffett, unknown, Arthur Riggs, unknown, Walter Kreger, Andrew Perry and the Rev. Clarence Shake.

Chapter Three

The Growing Years

In August of 1917, Mother and Dad took me to the Mc-Cutchanville School to register me for the first grade. Finally, the time had come when I could go to school and play with the other children, as Oscar had been doing for the last three years. The wait was over! Oscar was starting fourth grade, so I was never in the same classroom with him, which pleased me very much. He could not report to Mom and Dad about anything good or bad I might be doing, and that made me feel more grown up.

Our country school had three classrooms and three teachers. We entered the school building by going up several steps into a very wide hallway. On each side of the hallway were lockers to hang up our coats and leave our boots, if the weather was bad. The first and second grades were in one room on the left. Miss Swope was the teacher. On the right side of the hallway was the room for the sixth, seventh and eighth grades. Straight ahead was a multipurpose room that served as a classroom for the third, fourth and fifth grades; Miss Hubner was the teacher in that room. At one end was a stage with a curtain that could be opened and shut by hand. This was where we had our Christmas pageants, school plays, and other programs. It was also used for parent-teacher meetings and community affairs.

Miss Henry, the principal of the school, fired the coal furnace, was the head teacher, and taught the three older grades. We had a 15-minute recess in the morning and afternoon and an hour-long lunch period at noon. We usually sat at our regular desks to eat lunch if the weather was too cold to go outside to eat. The desks were screwed to a strip of wood that made them stationary; the chairs were also designed to stay in one place. The top of the desk was flat with an indention that held a bottle of ink; we dipped a pen into the ink to moisten the point for writing. We had a small space under the desk to store our books and other items.

If the weather was warm enough, we would go outside and sit at picnic tables in the school yard. Students rarely took very long to eat because the rest of the hour was social time or devoted to playing games. This was also the time we were supposed to take care of our bodily needs. If by chance this didn't get accomplished and one had to go during class time, it might have been embarrassing to ask permission to leave the room in front of all of the students.

For the first few days of school, Dad took me in the horse and buggy. We talked about how important it was to walk on the side of the road, particularly if we could hear a horse and buggy coming from either direction. He also cautioned me about never doing anything to scare the horse because I might get hurt. After the first week, I began to walk the 1½ miles to school in the morning and back home again in the afternoon. Every morning, when Oscar and I were getting ready for school, Mother was busy packing a nice lunch in each of our lunch boxes. Each box had an insulated bottle for a hot drink or soup. It would also contain a sandwich, apple, or other goodies.

When Mother had our lunch ready, Oscar and I would pick up our book bags and lunch boxes, and leave for school. Since we lived the furthest from school, we would start a few minutes earlier than our neighbors. We would walk together until we reached the Hornby home. As the girls came out of their house to join us, Oscar would speed up his walking. He was the only boy, so he wanted to get ahead of us. We walked past the rest of the Hornby farm, and up a long, steep hill. When we got to the top, the rest of the walk was on level ground. Mr. Hornby and Dad would take turns coming to get us in the buggy if the weather was rainy or really bad; they wouldn't have been working in the fields anyway.

During the winter of 1919, we had the biggest snowstorm I ever witnessed. Schools were closed for almost a week because we were snowbound. We had to shovel a path so we could reach the barns to feed the animals and milk the cows. The snow was even too deep to let the animals outside. We did not have big snow plows to clear the roads, as we do today. Usually a crew of men with their hand snow shovels would clear the roads so that people could get through, the milk trucks could pick up the milk, and the mailman could deliver the mail. Snow was piled so high on the sides of the road that we could not see anyone walking or driving their buggies on it. Finally, the snow started to melt, and things got back to normal.

Toward the end of my second year in school, I decided I didn't particularly like my teacher, Miss Swope. I felt that she never gave me very much help or took an interest in me. Later in life, I figured out for myself why this was probably true. Rumor had it that she wanted to date my brother, Arthur, and he wasn't interested. I'll never know if this was true or not, but I do know that I never felt that I got a good start in school. But I moved on to third grade in the next room.

One instance that happened when I was in about fourth grade, I shall never forget. Our classroom had a piano, and some of the boys were trying to move it where the teacher wanted it. It was accidentally pushed over backward and mashed the toe of a boy named Horace Moffett. His family lived close to the school. I didn't know all the details, but I learned that he developed an infection in his foot and died from it. I always felt so sad about this because I felt that with the proper care, his death at such a young age could have been avoided.

Miss Hubner, our teacher, was very kind and helpful. We spent a lot of time working on reading, writing (penmanship), and arithmetic. We had workbooks to help us develop muscle skills in holding a pen and pencil.

When I was in fifth grade, a music teacher visited our school to talk to the class about taking group music lessons on the piano. I wanted to sign up for lessons, and I requested permission from my parents right away. There was a piano at home, but I'm not sure when we got it, or why we had it. The piano teacher would visit once a week, and there were five in the group.

After about a year, the music teacher said that he would start teaching other instruments; I chose the violin. He loaned us the instruments to start with, but I wanted my own. With the help of my music teacher, my folks managed to buy a violin for me for $250; I still have it to this day. I think that practicing music helped me to perk up, and I took more interest in my other schoolwork. As I remember it, I always tried to do my best when I was studying and practicing, but I seemed to have a hard time getting it done, as we would always have work to do.

After getting home from school I would usually have a snack. Sometimes I would get a whiff of the bread that Mother was baking as I walked into the yard. I think she may have planned to have it come out of the oven about the time we got home from school. A slice of hot bread with homemade apple butter was always a special treat!

Every fall we made apple butter to use up the remaining apples left in the orchard. Making apple butter was a two-day job. The first day we would peel about two bushels of apples and get everything ready for cooking them. The next day we would prepare the copper kettle, which held about 20 gallons. The kettle had a rounded ball-shaped bottom that set on a round rack and held the kettle about 6 inches above the ground. We built an outdoor fire under the kettle to cook the apples. The kettle had a big wooden paddle with a long handle that fit on top of the kettle so that we could stir the apples. Throughout the day we added sugar and spices to the apples, which we constantly stirred until they turned a rich, reddish color. At this stage, the apple butter was ready to be put in pint jars and sealed. We would sell some, give some away to friends, and have enough to eat all winter long.

As I got older, I began to have more chores to do around the farm when I got home from school. I liked to collect the eggs from the hen house. We would do this twice a day, so the other chickens would not break the eggs when they got into the nests. A hen laid an egg every day, so if we had 50 hens, we could expect to collect about 50 eggs a day. Then we washed and packed the eggs so that they would be ready to take to town to sell on Saturday. We also took other things to sell, like surplus vegetables, fruits, and baked goods.

We could spend the better part of a day in town, particularly if we had to buy flour, sugar, and other things we might need. I was usually allowed to go with Mother, as I could help carry things into the places where we stopped. Most of the places were owned by relatives of our family who wanted to have fresh produce. I liked going on these weekend trips to town since they expanded my horizon. We would often stay and visit a few minutes with the relatives. I never quite understood how we were related, but apparently they were relatives on my mother's side.

Family Background

My mother was the ninth child, and was 8 years old when her father died. He was only 49 years old; Grandma Stahl was left to raise their family of 12 children, who were between the ages of 1 and 26. As I mentioned before, Gottleb and Barbara Stahl had lived in a large brick house on Stringtown Road, and this was where Mother lived when she was growing up. She would often point it out to me as we drove by on our way to town. In the early days, Stringtown Road was the main road to Evansville from where we lived.

When Grandpa Stahl died, Grandma started working with William Yokel in the partnership butcher shop business. This was a very difficult time for Grandma Stahl.

After seven years, she had help with her part of the butcher shop business when two of her sons, Ed and Oscar, began working at the butcher shop. Ed was three years older than Mother, and Oscar was five years younger. As soon as Oscar finished fourth grade, he started to work at the butcher shop. Ed had also been working at the shop, along with their father's business partner, Mr. Yokel. A number of years later, the Stahl brothers, Ed and Oscar, wanted to start their own butcher business.

The Stahls gathered outside the family home on Stringtown Road.

Ed, Oscar, and their sister, Lilly, decided to organize the Stahl Packing Company and separate from the Stahl/Yokel partnership. This was okay with Mr. Yokel. Evansville was growing, and there was room for both butcher shops to grow and prosper, which they did for many years. Aunt Lilly was the secretary/treasurer of the business. She must have done a good job because she worked there all of her professional days.

For many years, if we had the money, we would stop at my uncles' butcher shop to buy a piece of meat to have during the week.

Uncle Ed married Ada van Dusen and they lived on Stringtown Road. Uncle Oscar married Mayme Wittmer and they had two children, Glenn and Margaret Jane Stahl. They lived in Evansville. After our high school days, both Glenn and I went away to college, and then went our separate ways until we eventually ended up in Arlington, Virginia, where our families became very good friends. More about this later.

As I mentioned before, the Riggs family that moved here

from Ireland first settled in German Township, and then moved to a farm in the Bluegrass community.

My grandfather, Robert, and his wife, Ann, stayed on the farm and raised 12 children (six boys and six girls). Four of the boys (John, Simon, Richard, and Robert) and two girls (Mattie—after whom I was named—and Nettie) settled in the Bluegrass community or nearby.

Grandfather Robert Riggs.

Aunt Mayme, the oldest, and Uncle Ollie, the youngest, lived on Kratzville Road, and we lived about half way between them in McCutchanville. Three of the girls did not live to adulthood. I mention all of these details because we spent lots of Sunday afternoons going to visit our many relatives who lived nearby. There were four of us girl-cousins who were about the same age and liked to be together. These were the families that we went to visit most often.

I have great interest in my family's ancestry because of the times I sat on Grandpa Riggs' knee and listened to his wonderful story of traveling across the ocean to come to America. He was only 9 years old at the time of the trip. I enjoyed hearing all of the details that he shared with me. When he got older, he lived with Aunt Mayme and her family in her big three-story house on Kratzville Road.

The Bluegrass Methodist Church was the center of the Bluegrass community. A short distance from the church was a store where the families could buy supplies. Farmland surrounded this community center — several of my relatives lived up the hill from the church near the cemetery. Several years later the locals built another building next to the church for other community activities. Both buildings shared a very large lawn and parking space that were used by everyone living in the surrounding areas. The center was an ideal gathering place for community meetings and basketball games.

One yearly event that we always attended was the Christmas gift exchange. It was one of the highlights of my younger days. There would always be a tree about 20 feet tall, which was beautifully decorated. People would bring in strings of red cranberries and white popcorn to hang on the branches of the tree. Anyone who wanted to exchange gifts with other people in the community would bring their gifts and put them under the Christmas tree. Mother would always let me bring presents for my special girl-cousins. Santa Claus would distribute the gifts. Then we would sing Christmas carols, and every child would get a small bag of candy to take home. After Christmas was over, the organizers would take the tree out in the yard and let the birds eat the cranberries and popcorn.

I just got sidetracked in telling some interesting events of my life's journey, so, now back to school days.

Farm Chores

After hurrying home from school, I would have my snack. Mother would have things for me to do. Sometimes when the cows were not standing in the lane behind the barn, it would be my job to go back to the pasture and open the gate so they could start coming up toward the barn. The cows were smart enough to know that it would soon be milking time and their dinner time, as they were usually fed while we milked them. During this time they would stand perfectly still.

Another job I enjoyed was throwing down the silage. Every dairy farm had a silo, which was filled each summer with shredded green corn stalks to be used to feed the cows for the better part of the year. A cup of vitamin meal was put over the silage in the feeding trough. In this way, the farmer could enrich the cows' food, which in turn led to greater milk production and higher butterfat content. This last quality brought a better market price for the farmer, as the milk processing company could get more butter from the milk to sell.

To throw down the silage, I would climb to the top of the silo and enter through the opening for the top of several concrete doors evenly spaced down its side to allow access as the silage shrank in volume. I made my 25-foot climb up. When the silo had just been filled I could stand on the silage and look over the top of the silo and see for quite a distance. After absorbing the view of the surrounding growing fields, I would begin to sing! I always liked to imagine that each stalk of wheat or corn was a person and that I was singing to a very large audience.

Of course, this could only last for a few minutes because I had a job to do: throw down about a 2-inch layer of silage for the cows. This food landed at the base of the silo; Dad, or one of the hired men, would then scoop it up with a special shovel that had sides to it, and fill the long feeding trough. As we worked our way down the silo, the next door would be moved up to the open space above. One of the men folk took care of this. When Dad was ready to milk the cows, he would open the barn doors, and the cows knew which door to enter and which stanchion was their place to stand. We would come along and close the stanchion—which was like a collar around their necks—to keep them in place until we were through milking all of them.

Our herd of milking cows numbered 12 to 15, and we had about 30 gallons of milk to be picked up in cans each morning at a scheduled time by the milk truck. Dad let me help with the milking at a very early age. After he milked a cow, he would let me try to squeeze a little more milk out of the cows' teats. I could then feed this milk to the cats. Eventually, I was allowed to milk the cow from the beginning. Since the process of milking cows is so different now than the way we did it in the 1920s, I'd like to share a few details of how it was done back then.

We each had a three-legged stool and a two-gallon milk pail. First, Dad would go to each cow and wash its udder. We always milked a cow by sitting on its right side. We would gently pat the cow on the hip to let it know that we were there to milk. Then we would sit on the stool and lean our heads against the cow's side and squirt milk from each teat into the pail by squeezing them with our hands. We would soon set into a rhythm of left-right-left-right, and then front-back since a cow always has four teats. It was very important that we emptied the udder completely so that the cow would produce as much milk the next time. Often, Mother, Dad, Oscar, and I would all be milking at once. This time we spent together turned into sharing time—we would sing songs, talk about what happened at school that day, or what the plans would be for the next day. Dad, who was very good at math, would call out numbers, and Oscar and I would see who could give the correct answer first. He would also quiz us on addition, subtraction, and division, and we both developed strong skills in math.

A Love of Mathematics

Around this time in my life, I became excited about learning and studying mathematics. As I've mentioned before, the third, fourth, and fifth grades were all in the same room. In those days, the teacher taught all the subjects for each grade, including arithmetic, English, geography, penmanship, and music. This also meant she needed to plan different assignments for each grade. There were only eight to 10 students in each grade, and she knew the students and their families because she lived in the neighborhood. She would move from one class to the next, so we had study time in school to work on the next day's assignments. If we finished, we could listen to what the class was doing in the next grade.

Sometimes our class would have spelling bees. A spelling bee was a game that tested one's ability to spell. Players would line up against a wall and take turns spelling words. Those who misspelled a word had to sit down. The winner was the player left standing, meaning that the player was able to spell every word correctly. In preparation for our spelling bees, we were given a long list of words to study ahead of time. At night, we could have our parents call them out to us and help us learn them.

In fifth grade, the teacher determined that I was not ready to move on. Perhaps she was right, since my physical development was slow. After repeating fifth grade, I moved on to Miss Henry's classroom for the sixth, seventh, and eighth grades. Students in these higher grades were required to take a test in each subject and pass with a score of at least 80 to move on to the next grade.

At the end of sixth grade, a traumatic situation developed, as far as I was concerned. Miss Henry called me in to inform me that I didn't pass this important exam. My average for the year was 79½, but I needed a score of 80 to pass. Well, this made me very mad! I went home and told Mother and Dad. The next day my father went to school with me and talked to my teacher, but she held firm to her decision, and I was required to repeat my sixth-grade work. I made up my mind that I was going to just show her a thing or two! The next year, I started studying harder and getting better grades. Much later in life I decided that being held back that year was the best thing that could have happened to me.

The Challenges of Farming

I would like to express here what a challenging occupation farming was. One had to be able to plan his work for a year at a time, keeping in mind the amount of seasonal tasks that had to be done. In the spring, everything was focused on growth, and planting the seeds, and having the seeds on hand. Part of the preparation for plowing was to first haul the manure from the barnyard and spread it over the land. The next step in preparing a field for planting was to plow it. Usually, one horse was hitched to a plow, so the horse could pull it through the dirt. The plow was a large piece of metal fastened to a triangular wooden frame. The metal had a very sharp point in front and spread out in a triangular shape that was curved at the top, causing the dirt to fall upside down in a furrow. Then, a man would hold the wooden handles and guide the plow, so it would turn over the same amount of dirt while the horse pulled the plow around the field.

This meant that the ground was turned over so that the sod would be underneath the loosened soil. Then we would harrow the ground to knock up the clods. If necessary, we would use a disk to cut up the clods of dirt. Then the ground was dragged to smooth it off, or rolled, to pulverize the soil. This whole process prepared the ground for seeds that were to be planted. Sometimes what was being planted would determine how much work needed to be done in preparing the ground. The men usually did the plowing because it was hard work.

Dad always did the planting. The rest of the family would help with the other preparations. All of this took place in the spring when the weather was right for doing each job. It was important to do these jobs when the ground was not too wet or too dry. I did a lot of the rolling, dragging, and harrowing of the ground by having a team of horses hitched to the equipment. There was always a seat to sit on and drive around the field. Dad thought that the disking was too dangerous for me.

The primary crops that we planted were corn, hay, and wheat. Corn was planted in rows about 12 to 14 inches apart. A special piece of equipment was used to help cultivate the ground so that the dirt surrounding the plant would support the corn and help it grow tall and straight. Corn and hay were used partly to feed the livestock while the rest was stored for winter use. At times we planted clover for clover hay and soybeans for soybean hay. Soybeans contained a lot of protein, which was necessary for the animals' food, particularly for the milk cows. Wheat was a low-maintenance cash crop that was taken to the flour mills to produce flour and other wheat products. There wasn't much to be done to the wheat other than to watch it grow and pray that a storm wouldn't come along and knock it over! Wheat stalks were about the size of small pencils, and grew to about 3 feet 3 inches tall, including the wheat head that held the grain.

During the summer, a lot of extra jobs were done, such as cultivating the corn, tending the garden, and mending the fences. The women were preserving food for the family for the winter. During the growing season, we would often be doing the jobs to keep the farm looking neat and attractive, such as painting the barns.

Sometimes a circus would come to town. Because our barn was so close to the road, they would stop and ask to put a big sign on the end of the barn to advertise the circus. We would let them do it because they gave the family free tickets to see the circus. In the early part of the 20th century, a circus was a company of performers with their equipment that traveled around the country entertaining people. This was an exciting event because it also included trained animals such as monkeys, elephants, and horses. They had a very large oval-shaped tent with bleachers around the edge of the tent for their audience to sit on.

The farmer's plan, often interrupted by the weather, determined when all of these farming jobs got done. Oftentimes we couldn't do what we wanted to do at the time we wanted to do it because of the rainy weather. Other times, the weather was so dry that we were worried about having enough water to grow a crop.

Speaking of weather, I shall never forget a tornado that swept through southern Indiana when I was mowing the front lawn. The sky became very gray and dark. I was about 10 years old and wondered if the world was coming to an end. Next day, we heard the storm had swept away houses about 40 miles north of us. A few weeks later we drove to the storm area and saw that the floor and the basement were still there, but the houses and contents were nowhere to be seen.

Day by Day

I have been writing about the seasonal jobs on the farm, but now I need to write about the weekly and daily jobs.

Mother and Dad each had their separate jobs to do during the week. For Mother, Monday was laundry day, Tuesday was ironing day, Wednesday was quilting day and house cleaning, Thursday, we often prepared for visitors, and Friday was preparation for going to town on Saturday morning. After getting home, we would bake and prepare for Sunday. Sunday was church and rest. Dad's weekly jobs were gardening, planting and caring for his crops, milking the cows, feeding the animals, and so forth. Daily, we would have to prepare the food for eating, milk the cows, and feed the animals.

Monday was laundry day. Simple inventions from the period known as the Industrial Revolution affected how we did the laundry. We first started with our laundry tubs. Until I was about 9 years old, we did the laundry by using a washboard, our hands, and two tubs of water. The next development in washing equipment allowed us to wash clothes by pushing the handle back and forth as it swished the water around and agitated the clothes. On the side of the tub was a wringer, fastened on with screws, with a handle with two rollers that we cranked to turn. The clothes were put through the rollers that would push the water back into the tub. The clothes would go through the wringer into the rinse tub.

We repeated the process for the second rinse. Then the clothes were ready to hang on the clotheslines with clothespins. Light and dark clothes were washed and dried separately, so we had a line for each. These lines were put between two trees or poles that were secured into the ground. It was important to have them out from underneath any trees so the bird droppings did not spot the clean clothes. We gave the line extra support by using a moveable pole with a nail added to the side to help hold the line up in the air. The lines were positioned as high and as far apart as possible in order for the wind to go through the clothing. If one went for a drive, he knew that everyone was doing laundry on Monday because he could see clothes on the clothes lines. The real joy of doing laundry was in the fresh smell of clean, sun-dried clothing. It did not take very long for the clothes to dry on a nice sunny day, and they were usually taken off the line by evening. Some items of clothing were dampened down for ironing, and some were folded to wear.

Tuesday was ironing day. Before electricity, we heated a cast iron on the cook stove. It was a good idea to have a clean stove top and a testing rag, especially before ironing white shirts.

Wednesday was often cleaning day, and it was my job to clean the upstairs while Mother cleaned the first floor. Sometimes, Mother would call me and ask, "Are you about finished?" I would reply, "Well, pretty soon." The reason why I wasn't quite finished was because instead of cleaning, I would sit on the stairs and read a magazine like the Youth Companion. We subscribed to the Youth Companion for young people and the Saturday Evening Post, which always had illustrations on the front of it, many drawn by Norman Rockwell. I preferred reading over cleaning, but I cleaned eventually!

Once, when I was helping Mother clean the first floor of the house, I was cleaning around the desk. I opened the desk to put something in, and on the desk, I saw a printed sign that read "God is Love." At that point, I thought, "Oh, is that what we mean, and what we're talking about when we go to Sunday school and church?" This was one of my first revelations of what we meant when we talked about God: "God is love."

On Wednesdays, we cleaned and made our home presentable in preparation for relatives from Evansville, who would occasionally visit on Thursday. Mother's older brother, Uncle Ed, and his wife, Ada, would come almost every other Thursday, and we would always look forward to their visits. Aunt Ada was always dressed nicely, wearing a hat and gloves, as was the custom for ladies at the time. Many times we would give them fruit and vegetables from our garden to take home. I now realize that we probably should have been serving them a cup of tea and refreshments; I do not remember ever doing this. Most likely we didn't even have a copy of Emily Post's book of etiquette! Fortunately, this didn't stop them from visiting us.

I also remember a seamstress named Bertha Fosmeyer who would come, stay, and sew for us for two weeks every February. This was the time that Mother and I would each get a new dress to wear to church on Sundays. Once, when I was playing my favorite song on the piano, Bertha called out and said, "Oh, don't play that song; it was my mother's favorite song." Hearing it always made her think of her late mother and made her cry. After that, I always thought of that moment whenever I played that song.

This just gives you an idea of what we did each week. We were always busy sewing, canning, cleaning, or helping Dad outside; there was always so much to do. On Saturday mornings, we usually drove to Evansville to deliver produce. The rest of the day was spent preparing for Sunday. I must mention another important weekly event: how we took our baths after all the work was done on Saturday evening. First we had to carry the water into the kitchen and heat it on the stove in a copper boiler. Then, we would put a rag rug on the floor in front of the stove and then place one of our round laundry tubs on top of the rug. I was the youngest member of the family, so I was always the first to have a bath. Some hot water was poured into the tub and then cold water to make it comfortable. I would sit down in the tub and scrub myself and dry off in front of the hot stove. I'd also clean my teeth and wash my face at a small basin in a corner of the room, and run off to bed. The rest of the family would have a bath following the same routine. More water would be added to the tub to make it comfortable for the next person. Then the next morning the tub would be carried outside and emptied.

A Spanking

My first and only spanking that I can remember was a result of telling Mother a lie. She was so ashamed of me for telling a lie that she sent me outside to get a switch. When I came back into the house, she pulled down the blinds so no one could see. There would have been no one on the south side of the house able to look in at us, but she still pulled the blinds down. Then she had me bend over the dining table and switched me several times with the switch that I had brought in. The spanking did not hurt as much as Mother being so ashamed of me for telling a lie. I learned a profound life lesson that day.

At other times, while we were doing things in the house, Dad was outside cultivating corn, if needed, or working in the garden or the orchard.

Mother and I would can when the orchard's fruit was ripe. We had apricots, peaches, apples, pears, and plums. We made lots of jelly from the grapes and grape juice.

Dad was a very good gardener, and we had everything you can imagine in our garden. We grew horseradish that we could grind up and make a horseradish sauce to eat with meat. We also grew lots of sweet potatoes, corn, peas, beans, beets, etc.

Gardening was always an interesting project. When the sweet potatoes were planted, the land was moved with a hoe into ridges and the sweet potato plants placed on top of the ridge. The vines covered the ground, helping to keep the moisture in the ground. To plant the Irish potatoes, we would take the potato and cut it into pieces so that each piece had an eye on the surface. Then each piece was put into the ground, and the eyes would grow roots and then a plant. These plants would grow and produce more potatoes. Sometimes we would store the Irish potatoes in a pit for winter use. The sweet potatoes were usually stored on the floor on top of newspaper in our storeroom on the second floor. We canned many vegetables like sweet peas, corn, and butter beans.

Every year in the fall, we would butcher a pig. We had a smokehouse on the edge of the back yard. To butcher pigs, several neighbors would come together to help. They were killed and hung up by their feet (whoops, I meant the pigs!) and many different things were done in butchering pigs. We rendered the fat over heat and that made lard for cooking and baking all year, as well as the grease for our homemade soap. The different parts of the animal were cut in pieces, and we would cook the meat and put it in jars and can it. Sometimes we had pickled pigs feet, which were very good fried. The short part of the pig's legs and feet were cleaned and put in water to boil. When done, the meat would be picked off of the bones and added to the broth, which would thicken as it cooled. Other things were added for flavoring, but I cannot find the recipe.

Small pieces of meat were ground up and made into sausage. Mr. Effinger, one of our neighbors, was always given the task of flavoring the sausage because he seemed to have a knack for making tasty sausage. Some of the sausage was stored in bulk and some was put into the entrails. Now, let me explain that entrails are the large and small intestines of animals. The entrails were washed out, cleaned and then, with a meat press, filled with sausage. They would be tied off into strips of about 12 inches. Long strips of these were made and hung up on a rack. (For good detail, go to the history books on how that's done.) The hams were hung up in the smokehouse, and a fire was built so that the meat would be smoked with the salt used to cure the hams so that they would keep for a large part of the winter. It always amazed me that the weather was cold enough in the winter that we didn't have to worry about the food keeping, even though we had no refrigeration. The weather didn't seem to fluctuate like weather does now.

Making Hay, Threshing Wheat

Another interesting activity on the farm was harvesting the hay. First the field of clover or soybeans was mowed by using the mower machine close to the ground. The only time we would cut hay was when it promised to be sunny for the next few days.

After the hay was cut, it was allowed to dry. Then we would go along and turn the hay over, letting it dry on the other side. When the hay was cured enough, which meant being dry enough to be put in a hay loft, it was hauled to the barn. Let me explain that if the hay was still not dry enough it would heat up in the hay loft and could burst into flames and then the whole barn would burn down. It was very important to have the hay cured correctly before it was stored in the barn.

Once the hay was properly cured, it was raked with a horse-drawn piece of equipment that gathered the hay into piles. Then the wagon and the hay rack were brought in and loaded with hay. Men with pitchforks would throw forks full of hay up onto the wagon. The hay had to be properly arranged, and this was done by the person who was standing on the wagon; he (or she) was the loader. His job was to pull each forkful of hay toward the center line of the load and to overlap the piles as they were thrown up onto the wagon. The loader's goal was to form a nice rectangle of hay on the wagon that rose higher and higher. It was important to overlap the forks of hay so it would not slide off of the load. Otherwise, we had to start over.

After the hay was loaded, we took it to the barn, which had doors that opened on each end. We were now ready to unload the hay from the wagon and move it to the hayloft. An unloading fork was a special tool that was attached to a rope and dropped down over the load of hay from a track at the top of the barn. Because this was a pulley system, we attached the other end of the rope to one of our horses. When the hayfork was set, the horse outside the barn would start pulling on the rope that was a part of the pulley system. The hay was pulled to the top of the barn and along the track until it was dropped in the proper place in the loft. Of course, the whole purpose of growing clover and soybeans to be turned into hay was to feed the cows and the horses all winter long when they didn't have fresh grass to eat out in the fields. My father used to say that I could load as good a load of hay as anyone in the family. He praised Oscar too, but I remember my compliment especially.

Another activity that was planned in advance was harvesting the wheat. First, the farmer would cut the wheat when

49

it was ripe, which meant the stalks were dry and the grain had fully developed. Ripe wheat making waves in the breeze was a beautiful sight. When the wheat was ready, a special farm tool was used. It cut the wheat, which fell onto a canvas platform that carried it along. It was bundled, tied, and dropped to the ground. Then, six to eight bundles were stood up together and two spread on top to form a wheat shock. Then the wheat would stand in the fields shocked ready for the threshing machine to come. Owners of the threshing engine and machine would schedule their route so that all the wheat was threshed on every farm.

Threshing day was a big day at each farm. The women were in the house beginning to cook the noon meal for about 15 men. The men running the expensive threshing machine were trained to run this equipment. The threshing machine equipment consisted of two large parts: the threshing machine that separated the grains of wheat from the straw, and the engine that pulled the threshing machine from farm to farm and also furnished the power for running the machine.

While the men running this equipment were getting it ready to run, the other men were out in the field loading the wheat shocks onto their wagons to bring to the threshing machine. When all was ready, they would throw the bundles of wheat into the threshing machine and go back to the fields for another load.

The threshing machine separated the grain from the straw. The grain was put into burlap sacks and hauled to the wheat bin and emptied into the bin. The rest of the wheat stalks were blown from the threshing machine through a large round flexible tube that was controlled by ropes; it formed a nice round straw stack. The wheat in the storage bin needed to be stirred every once in a while as it was drying.

Soon after the threshing was finished, Dad would make an all-day trip to near the Wabash River, where they raised some delicious watermelon. This was our special fall treat. He would start out early in the morning with a team of horses and the wagon. He would bring back (depending on the size) about 10 for our family and as many more as people had ordered. Then we would lay our melons on top of the wheat in the granary, where they kept nicely until we were ready to eat them.

One thing that is very obvious to a farmer is that life on a farm is determined by the weather, so farmers learned to pray to God a lot because man doesn't control the weather! Then or now!

A model T Ford, the inexpensive car that put America on wheels. I drove an earlier model around the farm to distribute food and water to the men at age 11.

Driving at 11

Another important event in my life was driving a car at the age of 11. About 1921, my parents bought a Model T Ford, which cost about $300. It had four seats. To start the car, it had to be cranked. The crank was on the front of the engine. You had to get out of the car and crank it before you could start the engine. To crank it you had to set the spark plug and the gas lever in the right places. If it didn't start the first time, you would go around and change the position of the levers a little bit and try to crank it again. You kept this up until the engine started, but you didn't want to have too much gas or it would be flooded and then the engine wouldn't start. When it did start, you would run around and climb in behind the wheel, put your foot on the gas a little bit and get it running smoothly and then you could take off. At this early age, I had a hard time cranking it, and I never drove on the road.

When Oscar was old enough to drive and had saved up enough money, he bought a car with a rumble seat. It had two seats in front and instead of having a trunk, that space opened up into two seats where people could ride and was called a rumble seat. Because I was four years younger than Oscar, he would never take me along on any of his dates. But when he did have a date, he would always ask me to wash his car for him, which I did.

One of the last jobs in the fall was hauling the wheat grain into Evansville to the flour mill. The General Mills plant made various products from the grains of wheat. The flour was called soft wheat flour, which was used for making pies, cakes, and other pastries because it did not contain much gluten. Soft wheat was grown in the middle states in a warmer climate. Another kind of wheat was called hard wheat and was grown in the colder states like South Dakota and Minnesota. It contained sufficient gluten for making yeast bread. When yeast and hard wheat flour are moistened, the gluten begins to develop. Enough flour is added to the batter to form dough. To knead bread, we put flour on the kitchen counter and would fold and push the dough, turning and working it. The more the dough is kneaded, the more the gluten is developed, and the bread is a finer texture. Hard wheat flour also was used in making dumplings.

Another special time in my life was when I spent time on horseback watching the cows. Charlie, my horse, and Shep, my dog, spent many hours with me making sure that the cows did not get into the cornfield and eat the corn. All I needed to do was to call to Shep and say, "Bring the cows back." I would sit on Charlie's back and read a book or be thinking about my life. One time I prayed a very special prayer: "Dear Lord, I would really, really like to get married someday, and if possible, make it to a rich farmer, or a lawyer." Then I put the matter into His hands and I went on living a busy life.

Quilting Bees

The schoolhouse that we all attended was fairly modern for its day. Instead of being a one-room schoolhouse, there were eight grades and three rooms as I've talked about before. It was built on a piece of land that had two roads that came together in front of the schoolhouse. So, everything in the schoolyard in front of the schoolhouse was level and came to a point. This was where we played baseball. The land sloped down along the side of the building so the back of the school was at ground level. The social hall was underneath the classroom. A driveway across the school ground connected the two roads. The land went further down the hill into a valley between these two roads and this is where we could play. At one corner of that land was a crabapple tree that had little crabapples about the size of a marble, and we liked to collect those and throw them at each other. Sometimes we put them in our pockets and sometimes they got mashed and stained our clothes. The social hall was the recreation center for many community activities. Here is where the women of the Methodist Church would meet every two weeks for their quilting bees.

Making quilts was the way the Methodist women earned money for their mission projects. When the women arrived at the quilting bees, several of the quilts had already been put into the quilting frames—wooden poles made into a rectangle the length and width of the quilt. A quilt is made up of three layers: the lining, or backing, which is a solid piece of material and is attached to the frame first; the inner layer, which is a very thin cotton batting; and the third layer, which is the beautiful pieced top. These three layers were stretched and fastened to the quilting frame.

Quilting is a very detailed craft. The women would prepare the top layer of the quilt by sewing different colored squares of material together by hand. This was called "piecing the top." The women would piece the tops at home during their spare time from daily work. They took pride in what they were doing. This caused them to try to piece a beautiful top prettier than those of their friends.

Then it was time to do the quilting. Many women worked on one quilt, and several quilts were worked on at once. The women, with their needles and thread, would sit on the long sides of the quilt and go through the three layers to make a stitch. Many of them would try to make 12 stitches to an inch to be known as a good quilter.

Another form of textile art is called a crazy quilt because it used fabric scraps in an abstract pattern. Crazy quilts were not actually quilted but were lavishly embroidered to cover the seams and usually featured an embroidered spider along with many other symbols. This is more than 100 years old and was stitched in Abingdon, Illinois, by a friend of my husband's Aunt Winifred Miller.

This was recreation for the farm women. They had a great time talking and catching up on community news while they worked on the quilts. Sometimes they brought their young children with them. We children had fun playing underneath the quilts. The quilting frames were so made that the women could roll the quilt up when 8 or 10 inches had been finished.

They would continue this pattern of quilting and rolling toward the center from the long sides until they met at the center of the quilt.

The quilts were often sold before they were finished, particularly if the women had established a reputation of making beautiful quilts with lovely quilting. The better the work, the more they could charge.

Another popular community activity was the covered-dish dinner. This was truly a community affair: Families would bring their covered baskets with several different dishes. The food would be set out on tables and after saying a prayer, everyone would line up and pass around the tables and watch for special dishes people brought. Having these special dishes at the dinner made it a really great feast. It got so people would expect you to bring certain foods. I made very good angel food cake that was popular. Sometimes the children would wait and play outside until the adults had gone through the line and then they could come and help themselves. Before and after dinner, the men would play horseshoes, the children would continue their playing around the school, and the women would be cleaning up, visiting, and having a great time.

As I approach my teenage years, I must mention a couple of other things that were fun to do. I loved to go fishing at the pond that was back in our woods. Every so often, Dad would stock our pond with fish, and they would grow. I would find a long pole, and tie a strong string on to one end and a fishing hook on the other end. Since our pond was not very deep I tied a cork on the line about two feet from the fishing hook. This kept the fishing line from dropping to the bottom of the pond. Then I put an earthworm on the hook as bait, and cast the line into the water. When the fish starts to nibble on the bait, the cork starts bobbing up and down. At just the right time, one jerks on the line and maybe catches a fish on the end of the line and pulls it out. If the fish is too small, you carefully take it off of the fishing hook and throw it back in the pond to grow some more. But, if it's big enough, it is taken off of the fishing hook. You build a little fire, and cook the fish in the frying pan over the flames. Mmmm, that's good! All my life I have always loved to go fishing.

In the woods next to our property was a blackberry patch that grew in the shade, which kept the soil moist. The blackberries grew big and juicy. Before we would go into the blackberry patch, we would always put a rag soaked in coal oil (kerosene) around our ankles; that would keep the chiggers from crawling up our legs while we were in the woods. The blackberry pies were always a special treat.

The farm women always wore sunbonnets when they went outside to work. They were made of lightweight cotton to shade the face from the sun. In those days we never wanted our faces to become tan.

Chapter Four

The Teenage Years

To summarize my life up to this point: I was a very healthy child, and I remember very little about having any childhood diseases. But my brother Arthur seemed to see what his sister needed and always brought things to my parents' attention. One time he said to my parents, "Look, you must get Martha's teeth straightened." They did, and I have always been very grateful.

Another time, we were on our way to town on threshing day to get the meat for the noon meal. Since Arthur was 12 years older than I and was paying attention to the girls, he knew what I needed to be more stylish. When we stopped at the hairdresser's shop on Stringtown Road, he asked me if I would like to get my hair cut while he went into Evansville to get the meat. Whenever Arthur mentioned something, I usually went along with the idea. My hair was fine, not thick, and I had it braided and hanging down my back. I agreed to the haircut, if I could keep my braid.

Mother had given Arthur approval to take me to the shop, even though she was satisfied with just keeping her hair up in a bun on her head. The hairdresser put a string around my braid, close to my head, and tied it tight. Then she cut across the braid and finished cutting my hair. I took the braid home as a souvenir. I could take it out and compare it to my current hair color and see how it was changing. I kept it for many years. Everyone liked my new hairstyle, and commented positively about it. I never did grow it long again.

Growing up in a very caring and loving family was great. I never heard Mother and Dad fighting over anything. The only time that I heard Dad raise his voice was at the mules when they would not do what he wanted them to do. My parents did not want alcoholic drinks or playing cards in our home. They lived through a period when society was over-indulging and saw the evils of both—people getting drunk and gambling. But when Oscar and I were still young, Arthur persuaded them that a deck of bridge cards would not do any harm. Then we could play Hearts and other games.

Our family was living good, wholesome lives. I do not claim that we children were always perfect—once when Arthur and Ralph were in their middle teens, they helped carry out a prank on a neighbor's barn at Halloween. They took a wagon apart and assembled it on top of a barn. Of course this took a lot of energy and work, which they had fun doing, but the neighbor was not very happy to have to get it down again. When Dad heard about it, he scolded the boys and said he didn't want them to do anything like that again.

My short haircut.

One time, Dad had planted five acres of tomatoes for the cannery. A young man named Alfred came to the farm and asked Dad for a job. As he talked with him, Dad found out that this young man had run away from home. Dad said to him, "Son, you may work for me only if you will call your parents and tell them where you are." Alfred did call them, and he worked for us the rest of the summer. On one occasion he was picking tomatoes for the cannery and took his shirt off. He didn't realize that he was getting too much sun on his back and got a terrible sunburn so he could not work. It took several days before he could put his shirt back on and go out into the field to pick tomatoes. He really learned an important lesson, which I'm sure he never forgot. He finished working for us that summer and returned home. Then he enrolled at Purdue University, earned a degree, got a job working for the government, and eventually moved to Falls Church, Virginia, where our families saw each other socially.

As a Christian, Dad was really concerned about this young man and helped Alfred to get his life straightened out.

My last three years in grade school were very productive for me. I was enjoying my schoolwork, making good grades, and staying physically active. We had two recesses and an hour off for lunch. Our favorite game to play was baseball. We played a new game, with two new teams, each week. I was always among the first to be chosen because I was a very good baseball player. I know this helped me to have a better feeling about who I was. At recess and whatever time was left of our lunch hour after we'd eaten, we would play baseball. Each time we had to return to the classroom, we would remember the position we were playing and continue the game the next time we went out to play. Walking to school and playing games gave us the exercise we needed to survive the day's activities.

With brothers Oscar and Ralph Riggs.

4-H Leads to 4-Year Scholarship

I was a very busy girl outside of school. In addition to practicing piano and violin, I belonged to the sewing, baking, and canning 4-H clubs. 4-H was a national organization for the young people living on a farm, an important organization in our lives. 4-H means "hands, head, heart, and health." There were many different kinds of 4-H clubs. For women, there were the baking, canning, sewing, and home decoration clubs. The young men could raise many of the different farm animals and plants in their clubs.

Every summer, we would go to a 4-H camp to spend a week with our club leaders. We slept on straw mattresses on the ground in a tent that was big enough for 10 girls. These trips were very educational and exciting.

My main interest was the baking club because there were so many different things to bake. In the spring and summer of 1925, Mother let me do all the baking, but she was right there with me, teaching me how. I kept a record of everything I baked. I had quite an impressive summer working with Mother. Since we also had hired help on the farm for the season, I did a lot more baking than usual. I baked 1,200 biscuits, 600 loaves of bread, and more than 500 pies, in addition to cakes, cookies, kuchen (a sweet German coffee bread) and other treats.

The Vanderburgh County Fair was always before the end of August. Each baking club member had to keep a record of what she baked, write a theme about her summer's work, bake a loaf of bread, and enter all three in the county fair. Judges decided which entry received the first, second, and third prizes. The summer after I had completed seventh grade, I won the first prize in the 4-H Baking Club at the Vanderburgh County Fair.

All the first-prize winners in each of the 4-H clubs were expected to enter their work in the Indiana State Fair. Since two teachers in our neighborhood were planning on going to the State Fair, they were kind enough to enter my report, story, and loaf of bread on my behalf. We went to bed very early and got up at 3:00 the next morning to make the loaf of bread so it would be as fresh as possible.

The judges had to evaluate 100 loaves of bread and choose only one first-prize winner. In 1925, when I had just turned 14, I won First Prize for baking the best loaf of bread in the state of Indiana. I learned about winning first prize on Sunday morning when I arrived at church: Edna McCutchan, one of the teachers, wanted to tell me in person instead of using the public telephone. I could hardly contain myself when I heard the news; I was so excited!

I thought, "There must have been an angel hovering over my loaf of bread for it to be chosen for first prize." I shall always feel that my detailed records and essay that were entered with my loaf of bread were what helped me win because all of the 4-H bakers had to follow the basic recipe for a loaf of white yeast bread. There was nothing special about it, except that mine was chosen as best.

Winning was a tremendous moment in my life. The award for winning this "first prize" in the state of Indiana 4-H Baking Club contest was a trip to Washington, D.C., and a four-year scholarship to Purdue University. This was the first year the scholarships were ever given to women in the school of Home Economics. The biggest surprise to everyone, including me, was that I was only 14 years old when this happened.

All the state 4-H club winners were given a similar scholarship; the purpose was to develop leaders for the 4-H clubs. The trip to Washington, D.C., had been the prize awarded in previous years. A short time after the fair was over, we went on our trip. This was a great experience for me. As a girl growing up on the farm, we never once talked about taking a trip or going on a vacation. All the other winners were around 16 or 17 years of age, so you can imagine how well I, a rising eighth-grader, fit in with the group. I probably acted like a typical country kid at times: I remember swinging my feet while sitting on the corner of Herbert Hoover's desk. He was the Secretary of Commerce at the time.

I guess the greatest honor was having my picture in the Evansville Courier standing beside President Calvin Coolidge. Just remember that we did not have televisions at that time, so the newspaper was the only way to share the event.

Rep. Fred S. Purnell, left, introduced Indiana 4-H champions, including me, right, to President Calvin Coolidge, center, during the winners' trip to Washington, D.C., in 1925. I've kept this newspaper clipping from the old Evansville Courier for 87 years.

The state 4-H Club leaders and contest winners traveled by train to the nation's capital; only a few people were traveling by airplane in those days, so flying was not an option. It was in this year that Charles Lindbergh made his historic, solo flight across the Atlantic Ocean. According to accounts at the time, he at one point flew close enough to see fishermen in their boats. He called out to them "Directions to Paris?" They pointed him in the right direction, and he eventually arrived in Paris safely to a large crowd of people waiting to see him land. This was a very dangerous, adventurous trip. No one had ever tried anything like it before. This happened in the 1920s when radios were just beginning to be sold.

After settling into our rooms at the 4-H headquarters, we went sightseeing around town by trolley car, powered by electricity. Most of the ones at home, on the other hand, were pulled along the tracks by horses. They were gradually being switched over to electricity as it became available in the more remote areas.

As we rode through D.C., I noticed the Riggs National Bank as we rounded the corner of 15th Street and Pennsylvania Avenue NW. After noticing the name Riggs, I was curious to know if the president of the bank was a relative. Later I entered the bank to ask a teller and, of course, he didn't know. I wish I'd asked, instead, to speak with the president of the bank because I later found out that he did come from Ireland, like my grandfather. I concluded that he could have been a relative of mine, but so what?

The trip was great fun. We visited the White House and many other places of interest. Remember, we didn't have television then like we have now, so these sights were new to us. Of course, the most important thing about the whole event was the fact that Purdue University was willing to hold the scholarship for me until I was ready for college, which was five years later in 1930. Winning this contest at the age of 14 was both unique, a feat still unmatched by any Hoosier so young, and the most significant event of my whole life: I was one of the first—and the youngest person—to win a scholarship to Purdue University in the school of Home Economics, and the trip was my first time to go that far away from home for a week.

Back to Normal

After I returned home to Indiana, life became more "normal." I continued working at my first paying job, waiting on tables for family dinner parties held at the Hiwinkles' home. Dressed in my pretty white apron, I set the tables for guests. I learned how to set the table properly, fill the water glasses, and serve the food. Of course, there was always the clean-up after the dinner parties were over. After dinner, the guests would sometimes go into the living room and chat further into the evening. I helped put the food away and cleaned up the kitchen. There were usually one or two dinner parties a week. This meant that I had a very busy schedule the last year I was in grade school and my first few years of high school. I graduated from grade school in June of 1927.

Another 4-H club trip that I took was to Chicago in 1927. The International Harvester Company held a conference; over 800 4-H club members were present. The company, which made large farm equipment, paid for the conference. At that time, I was 16 years old and was very much taken by the large hats that the delegation from Texas wore, which I shall never forget. The conference was an educational conference to encourage young 4-H clubbers to become farmers. In the early part of the 20th century, the United States was very much an agricultural country; these young people came from farms from all over the country.

The 1920s were known as the turbulent years. Jitterbug dancing and the Charleston were becoming more popular. Society was changing after the soldiers came back from World War I.

What were my brothers doing during this time? Ralph, who had married Myrtle Newmaster at a young age, was working hard to support a family of five children and his wife. He was having a hard time making ends meet. He would come to our house, usually about the time we were eating dinner, and come in and sit down on the steps in the corner of the dining room. I could tell by the way he walked in and greeted us that he was going to ask Dad for some money. Dad would always share what little money we had. I learned at a very early age that this was the right thing to do. Sometimes this made me feel very sad because I knew I would have to do without something that I wanted. But from this vantage point in my life, I must say that Myrtle and Ralph raised a wonderful family of five children who all became productive citizens and a joy in our lives.

Arthur, my second brother, was attending Purdue University and graduated in 1925. Then he went on to attend Garrett Biblical Institute in Chicago, and prepared to be a Methodist minister. In April of 1928, he married Nancy Elliottt, who had just graduated from DePaul University with a degree in music. She specialized in organ music for the

64

church. They raised four children. The children all grew up and became professionals in their fields and contributed much to society.

Oscar and I were considerably younger than Ralph and Arthur. Oscar graduated from high school, and spent two years at Purdue University. He then decided to be a farmer, so he stayed home to work with Dad on the farm.

During the time that all my brothers were busy in their lives I, too, was very busy in mine.

Central High School

After we graduated from eighth grade, we had to pass another test before we could enroll in Central High School to continue our education. Miss Henry was a very good teacher, and her students usually scored among the best, and sometimes higher, than many of the city students. My test scores were ranked third in the county!

Painting by Evelyn Steinkuhl

Central High School.

I entered high school in the fall of 1927. Mother and Dad were very proud to take me into Evansville to Central High School to register me for the fall term. Going to high school ended up being a very different experience from grade school.

Here, I would have a different teacher for each subject and go from room to room for these classes. This was a very large school of students from throughout the county, and we had many activities. I qualified to play my violin in the high school symphony orchestra, which I thoroughly enjoyed.

I also was on the debate team, which was sponsored by the history teacher, Mrs. Bentley. This turned out to be the group that became my social activity in high school. I had my first crush on another member of the debate club. His name was Marus Risley. He had curly red hair, was moderately handsome, and liked to talk about his hobby. I was not very interested in his hobby, which was being an undertaker for animals. We remained friends, but I did not find him very interesting to talk with.

To get to high school, we had to be ready to catch the school bus early in the morning, which meant that I could no longer help with the morning chores on the farm. A few evenings, I stayed after school for special activities such as the debate team. Then I would have to take the late bus home. It took about 40 minutes for the five-mile route. This also meant that the country students could not participate in many of the evening activities at high school. One year it was decided by a vote that all the girls would wear the same pattern of dress to school, like a uniform. It was a medium tan washable material. Many of the girls made their own dresses, but others had to have dressmakers make them. I made my own. This dress code lasted for about a year. The idea was to keep the girls from dressing up and spending a lot of money on their clothes. But it did get across the idea that girls were not to dress up to go to school. They needed to be neat, clean, and comfortable.

Since I had won my scholarship to Purdue University in 1925, I had made up my mind that I would go through high school in 3½ years by going to summer school. Therefore, I made up one of the years that I lost in grade school.

In my junior year of high school, I had an English teacher by the name of Miss Gerst. Her assignment was to write a theme on any subject that we chose. I decided to write on that little word "if." I spent a lot of time writing about this theme and thought that I had done a pretty good job. She wrote "trite" on my paper and put a C for my grade. Whether I deserved that or not, I will never know, but it affected me for many years because I felt I could never write anything worth reading. But now here I am trying to write a book because I have an exciting story to tell. These were very busy and productive years in my life.

The Great Depression

Before I close this chapter of my life, I want to mention other things going on in the world around me and my family. The United States began as a farming country. During the 1920s, the Industrial Revolution was getting a good start: Small cities were beginning to develop near manufacturing sites. Then railroads were being built, cars were being made in factories. Society was changing, but you can read about it in your history books. Then in 1929, the Great Depression hit our country. This was during my senior year of high school, in October. The financial system that had developed collapsed completely—-the bank doors closed and no one could get any money out of the bank. We never got a cent of our money that we were saving for taxes. Fortunately, I had some money I earned from my first job; instead of putting it into the bank, I had saved it myself. Had I put it into the bank, I would have lost it all.

Farmers fared the best during the first few years because we always had food to eat. We would take our produce into Evansville to sell to our regular customers, but they would not have money to pay us every time. We would let them have the food because we knew that they would pay us when they did get some money. We needed money to buy sugar and flour, but everyone was in the same situation, so we learned to share and care for each other.

I've always cherished the many times that my friend Alice George and I spent Sundays together. We would go home with each other after church. Sometimes we would play croquet. When we were tired of being outside in the sun, we would go in and play Parcheesi and other games. Since she was an only child, and I was the only girl in my family, we filled a need in each other's lives. When I was held back in sixth grade, Alice was still in the same classroom with me. But, I knew that she would head to high school before I did. Our friendship was a great motivator for me to push ahead in my studies.

We had a medium-sized sassafras tree that grew partly on our farm, and partly on the Hornbys' side of the fence line. One of the first things we did as spring approached was to focus on our usual sassafras tea. Each time we wanted a cup of this blood-thinning brew, Dad would dig up the tender roots and put the woody pieces into a pot of water, then boil and serve it.

In the fall, when we had apples left in the orchard, we would dry them in the sun. We first peeled the apples and sliced them into about eight pieces. Then we would lay paper on the roof of the chicken house and put a clean cotton cloth on top of the paper. Next, we would spread the apples on top of the cloth and let them dry in the hot sun. We used the chicken house roof because it was slightly sloped. When the apple slices were thoroughly dry, we would store them in a container. In the winter we would boil the apples in water and use the juice to make apple dumplings. This was one of our favorite desserts, served with a little sugar, cinnamon, and milk on top.

As I remember, this is the recipe for the dumpling batter:

Dumpling Batter

2 cups flour
4 tsp. baking powder
½ tsp. salt
About ¾ cup milk or a little more to make a soft dough.

Drop dough into the boiling water that was used to cook the apples. Boil covered for 5 minutes. Serve in dessert bowl with cooked, sliced apples on top. Sprinkle with sugar and cinnamon, and pour a little milk on top.

Another special time was Memorial Day. To get ready for Memorial Day, we would go out in the yard the morning before and cut flowers (mock orange, peonies, lilac, bridal wreath spirea, and any other flowers in bloom) to make beautiful bouquets for 12 to 15 graves at the cemetery. The morning of Memorial Day, we would go to the cemetery and distribute the bouquets on the graves of relatives and family. I remember that Mother always had one for me to put on the grave of my baby sister, who had died at birth. Many other people would be at the cemetery decorating the graves of their relatives. Then we would walk to a nearby knoll that had places for people to sit on benches near a stage. We had about an hour's program singing patriotic songs, hearing patriotic speeches in honor of our veterans, learning about the importance of family, and paying tribute to our ancestors. This is one of the special holidays that we celebrated during the year. Besides funerals, this was usually the only time we went to the cemetery. This was also one of the few holidays that everyone stopped their routines to observe.

We never took a vacation because there were always daily chores to do on the farm. Until I was 10 years old, we traveled by horse and buggy, which meant that we could not travel very far from home.

One thing that my family loved to do was to sit and watch the airplanes land, especially in the evening when the red lights were on all around the edge of the airport. Since the airfield was in the shape of a triangle formed by a railroad track and a public road coming together, it looked like a Christmas tree all lighted up.

I graduated from high school in June of 1930 in the largest class that had graduated from Central High School. I was 19 years old and spent the summer getting ready to go to Purdue University to use my scholarship. Now I will turn my attention to writing about the next step in my life: going to college.

Chapter Five

The College Years

After graduating from high school in 3½ years, I was ready to go to college. As you will recall, I won my scholarship to Purdue University in 1925; it was held for me until I was ready to attend. Purdue University was known primarily as a land-grant university. Land-grant universities were federally sponsored institutions designed to help rural young people acquire a higher education in the techniques of farming to equip them for life on the farm. Soon the mechanical and science arts were added to the courses offered. It was understood when I won the scholarship that I would be enrolled in the School of Home Economics and study to be a teacher of home ec. The purpose of the scholarship was to train women to be 4-H Club leaders.

The summer after I graduated from high school, we made a trip to West Lafayette, the Purdue campus, to register me for the fall term at the university and to gather information regarding what I needed to do to be ready to start my college education. We found out that I could stay at the co-op house, just a half a block from the Home Economics building where I would be attending classes. After the visit, we went home to prepare for this important change in my life. I made clothes and made a list of all the things I would need for living away from home. I still had the small job of serving at dinner parties to earn money to help cover expenses for my first year at school. This was the same job that I had during high school.

In the fall when I arrived at the co-op house, I had been assigned a room on the first floor next to the kitchen. I was probably lucky to get a room here, even though it was not the most desirable one in the home. There were 25 women who boarded in the house, but little time to get acquainted with all of them. A majority of the women were upper classmen and also home economics students. Only a few were freshmen, probably because this was the first school year after the Great Depression began in 1929. Another young lady, who was also a freshman, was assigned to room with me.

As residents of a co-op house, it was our responsibility to share the housekeeping duties among us. We did "co-operate" and kept the house in order. We always had group study hours every evening from 7 to 9. During this time we could study because it was a designated quiet/study time.

After 9 p.m., many of the girls would come to the kitchen to socialize and make hot chocolate and cinnamon toast. I liked both of those treats very much and would have a hard time returning to the study sessions as long as they were in the kitchen. Over the course of my first year I had the unfortunate experience of gaining 20 pounds! It was also unfortunate that the co-op house was so close to the Home Economics building that I didn't have a very long distance to walk to class. I should have known better. But, it was a fun time because I didn't realize what was happening to me.

I was soon rushed by a sorority. Before I decided, I discovered the cost and experience of such a lifestyle was too much, and I refused the invitation. I soon became very active in the Purdue Independent Association Group, where I was able to develop leadership skills because I was not living in an "organized" house. I was also able to be active in athletic pursuits. I was captain of the women's field hockey team and excelled on the table tennis team. I also became an expert marksman in riflery; I could consistently hit the target! Archery was fun, too; I still have my bow. I was also a member of the Women's Athletic Association. All of these activities probably helped me be chosen to be a Gold Pepper in my junior year, which I'll explain later.

I'm fourth from right in this Debris yearbook photo of the Purdue women's field hockey team.

To help keep the expenses low, I made it a habit to use second-hand books. Remember, these were the Depression years, so there was little money to spend on school supplies and other expenses. And, as you can imagine, I had quite an adjustment to make because this was my first time away from home. The only break from classes was for the few days between semesters, and for Thanksgiving, Christmas, and summer. My transportation back and forth to college for these vacations was usually with other students who lived in my hometown area.

At that time there were no washing machines in the co-op house, and the public machines on campus were too expensive to use. The only way to have clean clothing was to send home dirty laundry in canvas bags and to have it sent back cleaned and folded. These bags had a unique labeling system: one flap had my school address on it, while the other flap had my parents' address. Depending on which direction the bag and the clothing were headed determined which flap was left on top before the bag was strapped closed.

Physical education was my minor at Purdue. I'd always been very active during my grade school and high school years, and I felt that this was a suitable choice. For my love of mathematics, I took as many courses as I could work into my schedule. I had no choice as to what major I was choosing because I'd earned my scholarship in preparation for teaching home economics. That was the coursework I had to take in order to prepare for a position in 4-H Club leadership.

Class time was divided among sewing, cooking, canning, and other household duties such as budgeting, child training, and planning a home. The general education courses such as math and English helped complete our well-rounded education.

One of the hardest things about school was meeting the physical education requirements. To meet these requirements, we had to swing on rings hanging from ropes across the length of the gym. We also had a swimming pool and had to learn to swim enough to be able to float and handle ourselves in water. I learned enough skills to meet these requirements, but to this day I've never really learned to swim. Naturally, I lost the 20 extra pounds in the process and by staying active in the gym.

The Memorial Gym, which housed the swimming pool, was dedicated in 1909. It was built to remember 16 Purdue football players who died in a train wreck in 1903. Since swimming was not available to many of us from farming areas, Purdue took the lead in promoting this activity. By 1913, the campus was involved in inter-collegiate swimming and diving.

The Wesley Foundation

Purdue's population was fairly large, with a 10-to-1 ratio of men to women. Since these were Depression years, no one had extra money to spend on social activities, and there was very little dating. There were a large number of fraternities and only a few sororities. In my search to find a church to attend, I found information about the Wesley Foundation in the school's handbook. This organization was sponsored by the Methodist Church, and it became my social center on campus. There was always something going on, particularly on weekends.

Two sponsors of the Wesley Foundation were Harry and Sally Cleaver. The foundation was located in a large house on State Street, and the student activities took place on the first floor. The pastor and his family lived on the upper floors. One of my favorite activities was hiking to Sleepy Hollow with the group on Sunday afternoons and evenings. We would hike about 1½ miles to a wooded area, where we built a bonfire, roasted hot dogs and ate them with fresh apples. Then we would make "s'mores" by roasting a couple marshmallows, and putting them between two graham crackers and a very thin bar of Hershey chocolate. These were so good. We also played table tennis and other games at the Wesley Foundation, just to be together and have fun.

The first year of college passed without any significant events. Most of the time was spent going to classes and getting adjusted to living away from home. The co-op house was not necessarily expensive, but I needed to find a cheaper place to live. Mr. and Mrs. Cleaver suggested that I live with them after the summer break and work for my room and board. This was a great arrangement, and we became very close friends. Their son, Dale, was in his preschool days, and was easy to take care of. I was always there as his babysitter when his mother and father went out in the evenings. I was often there for mealtimes and in the evenings, when I would study after he had gone to sleep. I also helped clean up after meals and washed dishes.

In my sophomore year, the Wesley Foundation conducted a Bible study discussion group made up of a handful of men and women. Every Tuesday evening we would meet to discuss matters pertaining to the church, the Bible, and college life. This was especially important for me because it exposed me to a diverse group of students with different outlooks on life, the importance of God and having faith, as well as how to live a more Christian life. This was the first time that I had been in an adult group where we were discussing things about the Bible, trying to understand what had been written. The in-depth questions helped me to broaden my outlook; they were very different from the Sunday School lessons I had sat through as a young child, or when I passively accepted what the pastor of our church would preach. I was beginning to decide who God was in my life, and how much of my life I would give to Him.

The friendships that I developed during these meetings lasted beyond the college years. Two of the members, Phil Aylesworth and George Wall, who were graduate students, seemed to have a deeper knowledge of the topics we covered, probably because they were older. A few years later, our paths crossed again when we were all living in Arlington, Virginia.

That June, I spent a week babysitting my brother Arthur's two children. At the end of the spring semester, I went to his home in Wisconsin. Because Arthur was a Methodist church preacher, both he and his wife, Nancy, wanted to go to the statewide church conference held each year in June. I went a few days early to get acquainted with the two children, Elliott and Nancy C. Elliott was about three years old, and Nancy was about one year. Since I did not have a lot of practical experience with children this young, this was a new experience for me. Generally speaking, everything that was routine such as meals, naps, and going to bed, all went very well, and we managed to hold the fort.

After the children's naps in the afternoon, I would usually try to take them on a walk. This was not always easy: Elliott was a very active tyke, and Nancy was in the baby carriage. Elliott would like to run way ahead and try to hide behind a tree. My concern was that he would forget to stay on the sidewalk and run out into the road. This was not good, so I would insist on having him in his walking harness for safety reasons. I will have to admit that I was glad to see their parents come home. On the day of their return, I watched out the window at each car coming down the road, hoping it was theirs! Although I was learning the theories of child-raising, I discovered that the practical application was a different story.

A highlight of my junior year was when the Wesley Foundation put on a play called the "Bishop's Candlesticks." A pair of silver candlesticks played an important part in the play. There were three characters: the Bishop, played by Howard Farrington; the Sister, who I played; and the Maid, played by Marjorie Reinoehl. Backstage there was an electrician and a property manager as well as our pastor and his wife. On Sunday afternoons, we would pack up the set and costumes and travel to local churches in the area and perform this play. During that year, we performed a total of 20 times. After each performance, a collection was taken and given to the Wesley Foundation. Afterwards many of us kept in touch with each other for the rest of our lives. The Bishop and the Maid—Howard and Marjorie—married shortly after graduation.

It may be interesting for you to know that as a child I was very shy, and I never wanted to get up in front of anyone. I credit my years on the debate team in high school for helping me to be more relaxed about performing in public.

Harry and Sally Cleaver had moved to the East Coast, so during my fourth year at Purdue, I lived with five other girls in a private home owned by Mrs. Pontius, the widow of a former Purdue professor. I earned my room and board by babysitting her two little girls and doing light housekeeping. The house was very close to the Home Economics building where I spent most of my time.

Edith Jones was my roommate in a small room that was really an enclosed porch with French doors leading into the living room. We each had a desk, a bed, and closet space, so it was generally very cramped. When I began struggling a bit in one of my math courses, I asked Edith, a science major, if she would help me, but she refused to help me directly. Instead, she would ask me questions, enough to help me get the point. The idea was to let me figure it out myself, which I eventually did. She would be fast asleep while I was still struggling to get my assignments completed. Fortunately we both passed the course and remained good friends for many years afterwards. All of the girls in the house kept in touch after graduation. We had all attended activities at the Wesley Foundation when we each had time.

University Groups

To summarize my university days, I'd like to point out a few honors I received, and some of the organizations of which I was a part.

At this time in women's university education, there were few organizations that recognized scholastic achievement. A booster organization for Purdue women, the Gold Peppers, required some scholastic achievement as well as prominence in other campus activities and leadership skills. I was honored to be one of the 15 women chosen in their junior year to be members of the Gold Peppers. During our senior year, we represented all of the co-eds on campus by supporting and carrying on the sports traditions of the university, and encouraging the younger women to be a part of them too. Each member of the group received a wooden paddle engraved with a gold pepper; I still have mine to this day. We wore black berets with a gold pepper insignia on them all around the campus during our senior year.

Here is what the Debris yearbook had to say about Gold Peppers:

"Attendance at all athletic events, including the pep sessions preceding football games, is one of the numerous traditional activities of Gold Pepper members. Its members lead the Derby Day procession, are accorded seats in the front row at all the basketball and football games, and have built up the custom of selling gold and black balloons at the major football games of the season. A contribution was made this year to the Dean Carolyn Shoemaker memorial fund for the aid of financially distressed students."

I was also a member of the debate team, Debris staff, the Women's Home Economic Society, the Purdue Independent Association, Purdue Sports Women, varsity hockey, volleyball, baseball, and riflery teams, the Women's Athletic Association, YWCA, the Wesley Foundation Players, and the Wesley Student Guild Association. I don't know how I found the time to do all of this while working for my room and board, but I was obviously very busy.

My family was also busy in their lives: By the time I was in college, Ralph and Myrtle had five children, four boys and one girl. Mother and Dad bought a small farm, a few miles from Darmstadt, where Ralph and his family lived and worked for a number of years.

In 1925, Arthur graduated from Purdue University and went on to Garret Biblical Institute in Chicago to prepare to be a minister in the Methodist church. He finished his graduate work and soon married Nancy Elliott on April 11, 1928. Nancy had just graduated from DePaul University's School of Music. Their wedding took place in Chicago. I was invited to stay in Nancy's parents' home and share a room with Nancy's sister, Edith. I shall never forget seeing her dresser drawer with about 12 pairs of shoes lined up in order. I couldn't believe that any person owned that many pairs of shoes! Arthur and Nancy raised a family of three boys and one girl. They, too, became successful professionals in their chosen fields.

My free, four-year scholarship to Purdue was one of the "Greatest Blessings" of my life. I shall always feel that my "Guardian Angel" was guarding my loaf of bread when the judges awarded it first prize in Indiana's 4-H Club baking contest. This was the only reason that it was possible for me to go to college during those Depression years.

During my senior year, my brother Oscar and Harriet McCutchan were engaged to be married. Their wedding day was January 30, 1934. This was during my last semester of college, and I lived with them for a short time just after graduation.

At this time, Dad was 68 years old and Mother was 59 years old. The plan was that Oscar and Harriet would take over the running of the farm. Mother and Dad were able to buy a bungalow in McCutchanville across the road from the school ground where we all went to school. There was just one big problem: The house would not be ready for them to move into for three or four months. Arthur and Nancy invited Mother and Dad to visit them in Wisconsin until the house in McCutchanville was ready for them to move into. This bungalow was just right for Mother and Dad to live in as they started their retirement years. They were settled in their new home before I graduated from Purdue in June of 1934.

My brothers Arthur, Ralph and Oscar and me with our parents, Minnie and William Riggs, seated.

Before I finish writing about college days, I must tell about my one college romance. In the spring of my sophomore year, I met Jim Craig. He was a student in the School of Forestry. He came to the Wesley Foundation for some of the weekend activities such as our hikes to Sleepy Hollow on Sunday evenings. During the following summer, he went to northern Canada to work in connection with his school activities. He was in a forest of birch trees. We had fun writing letters to each other. He would peel off a thin layer of bark and write me a letter using the bark for his letter paper. We continued to write all summer. We saw each other when we came back to school in the fall; he was in the sophomore class, and I was in my junior year. He gave me my first kiss, but I guess I did not respond with very much enthusiasm, and we started to drift apart. We both became busier in our schoolwork.

As we approached the time for graduation exercises, I was feeling very grateful and humbled for having won the four-year scholarship, recognizing that it could have been someone else standing in my place at graduation. However, I was very happy and joyful that I was able to wear the cap and gown and walk across the stage to receive my degree. Again, I was so grateful to have a college education because it changed my life. My folks weren't able to spend money on our schooling. And at the time, women weren't always encouraged to pursue higher education.

Mother and Dad, Minnie and William Riggs, in 1938.

In 1934, 51 of us graduated from Purdue's School of Home Economics. Four years after the Great Depression began, there were still not many jobs available, and only one person from our group had signed a contract for employment.

As a Purdue University graduate, 1934.

Chapter Six

The Post-College Years

After graduation, with no prospects of a job, I felt at a loss as to what I was going to do. I really didn't want to be hanging around with Mother and Dad. If I remember correctly, I sat down and wrote a letter to Sally and Harry Cleaver to tell them of my situation. During my junior year, Mr. Cleaver had taken a job working for the Department of Agriculture in Washington, D.C. Sally wrote back saying that they didn't have much room, but that I was invited to stay with them until I found a job. I gave this considerable thought because it was a big decision for me to make. But after reasoning that it was worth a try, I began to prepare for my trip to the nation's capital. It seemed like a good opportunity to broaden my prospects for a job. Excited about the idea of going to Washington, D.C., I made preparations to travel there by train.

In October 1934, I left home for Washington, D.C. I loved seeing the beautiful trees in their fall colors as I traveled across the Appalachian Mountains. It was a little scary venturing out into the world on my own, but the trip developed into an exciting adventure that "lasted a lifetime."

Upon arriving in Arlington, Virginia, I found the Cleavers living in a two-bedroom, one-bath bungalow on Jackson Street. There was a porch across the front and a screened porch in back. They now had two children under five years of age. The only place for me to sleep was on the screened-in porch. This was fine in the fall, but I also slept out there all winter. We'd put newspapers between the mattresses as well as the blankets that covered me. Sometimes when it snowed, the snow would sift through the screen onto the porch. I managed to survive, though, and stayed healthy all winter. It was nice to be with the Cleavers again.

I soon found a job making salads at the Agriculture Building cafeteria. I rode with Harry to work every morning. He drove through Fort Myer where, at the time, there were no gates. We passed Arlington House, also known as the Custis-Lee Mansion, which sits on a hill overlooking Arlington Cemetery, the Potomac River and Washington. It was a beautiful drive as we continued down Constitution Avenue to the Agriculture Building on Independence Avenue. I soon decided to look for other jobs with better pay because I realized that the Cleavers didn't really have room for me to stay with them. I was willing to do anything (sleeping on the porch, for example) to be with friends in this big city.

In the spring, they told me that they thought I should find a room near a church, in Washington. They really didn't have enough room for me, but I felt sad and hurt when they asked me to move because I didn't feel ready to go; it was like a bird being pushed out of the nest. I knew that I had to eventually stand on my own two feet.

Foundry Methodist Church

By that time, I'd found another job working at the Dodge Hotel near Union Station and the Capitol building. I was working in the gift shop. Johnny Andrews, a Purdue graduate and a friend of the Cleavers, introduced me to the Foundry Forge, a group of "young professionals" who attended the Foundry Methodist Church on 16th Street Northwest. Shortly after realizing that I had to move out, I began a search for a room near Foundry Church. After having worked my new job for several weeks, I had a little more money to rent a room. I found a room for rent at 15th Street NW and Massachusetts Avenue, a short distance from the Foundry Church.

After I rented the room, the landlord of the property informed me that I'd be staying with three or four other girls. Remember, these were still Depression years and money was tight. Despite my uncomfortable feelings, I went ahead and moved in. Johnny Andrews and the Cleavers helped me move what few things I had. I soon knew that I would have to look for a better place to live. I was a bit wary of the other women. I'd go to bed every night with the little bit of money I had in my possession hidden inside my pillowcase to protect it while I slept. The few weeks at this location was a very uncomfortable period of time for me, but I kept busy with working and attending Foundry Church. I just kept praying that nothing terrible would happen to me, and I prayed for God to help me find another room!

At Foundry Church I found a wonderful group of young professional men and women. They met for social and spiritual activities and called themselves the Foundry Forge. These young people came to work for the government to help the new president get this country over the Great Depression. In 1932, Franklin D. Roosevelt had been elected president, and many events were taking place in Washington, D.C., so the young people at Foundry Forge were a wonderful group to be with.

I was so fortunate to meet a young lady from Ohio by the name of Mary Pontius, unrelated to my Purdue landlady, who also was looking for a roommate. She came to Washington to be secretary to a congressman from Ohio. After finding out that we were both from the Midwest and that we had a lot of interests in common, we decided to find a room together. We looked for a room close to the church, but finally located one on Lamont Street. It was in a private home between 16th Street and Rock Creek Park. It was such a blessing to find another room so I could move out of the situation I was in. It was also wonderful to have a roommate with whom I could do things.

At work, Mary and I were on the opposite sides of the United States Capitol. I worked at the Dodge Hotel, which was on the northwest corner, and Mary was working at the congressman's office on the south side. I liked working at the hotel gift shop. We had to use the streetcars for our transportation because it was too far to walk. Later, when I looked back over my account books from this time, I observed that I had never bought a pair of new shoes; I simply had my soles and heels replaced on my old shoes.

While working at the gift shop, I was selling a lot of cigarettes. I sold so many cigarette packages that I began to think, "I wonder what I'm missing by not smoking. Everybody seems to be doing it." So one day, I decided to buy a package of cigarettes, which I knew was against my parents' wishes. I felt that I should experiment and decide for myself. That day after having bought myself a package, I left the hotel and walked over toward the Capitol. I really didn't want anyone seeing me trying to smoke. I took a cigarette out and started lighting it up. The match lit up but quickly went out, so I had to light another. I was feeling very guilty about doing this, and as I walked along I saw a trash can and made the greatest decision of my early life: I would not try smoking. I threw my cigarette pack into the trash can and never again thought of trying it. Looking back from my present situation, I feel that that decision I made on the steps of the Capitol building was one of the greatest decisions I made in my life. Then I began to feel proud of myself because even though I never told them about it, I knew that my parents would be happy to know that I had made this decision.

One of the things I did while looking for work was to inquire at the school board about a teaching job in the District. They pointed out to me that I would still need to take a course in mathematics in order to qualify for a position. Now that my life was a bit more under control, I felt that I should get prepared to teach, so I took a correspondence course in order to qualify for a teaching position. This turned out to be a good investment in my future days, even though I did not get a job teaching in the District.

In my search for a better job, I applied to the Home Service department of the Washington Gas Light Company. Since I was a Home Economics graduate, I qualified for this job because I knew how to cook. The task of an employee of this department was to visit the homes of people who had purchased a new gas range and teach them how to use it. For a while I had worked at Kann's Department Store, which sold gas ranges. When I was hired by Washington Gas, it was part of my job to check the ranges to see that the flames were adjusted properly and that the oven tested at the right temperature for baking. The company provided cookbooks for us to give to the customers. There were about six women in this department headed by a supervisor by the name of Miss Sheldon. Each of us had a car to drive all over Maryland, Washington, and Virginia servicing gas ranges in the metropolitan area. Many times we didn't know whether we were going into a home where white people or black people lived, and sometimes they were mixed-race homes. This might have bothered some people, but not me; I visited homes in all areas of the District.

Foundry Church was a wonderful place and the center of my social life. There were about 125 young people in the Foundry Forge, led by the Rev. Ford, a retired pastor. This place was on the corner of P and 16th Streets NW next to the church. It was a large residential mansion, and on the second floor was a beautifully decorated room where we'd often have dances on Friday evenings. Other activities included weekend outings to the mountains. Many of the young women in this group belonged to a Sunday school class that met weekly in the church. Miss Spencer was our teacher. We studied the Bible and had lots of good discussions. We shared a lot in common, growing together spiritually and making many friends. We'd then attend church at 11 o'clock. Our pastor, Dr. Harris, was also chaplain for the United States Senate.

As you can imagine, these were very busy times. I was writing to my parents every week, taking a correspondence course, socializing at church, dating a little bit, and having a great time. Johnny Andrews and I would often visit the Cleavers on the weekends. I continued keeping in touch with the Cleavers; they were like an extended family for me.

Here I would like to express my appreciation to Harry and Sally Cleaver for all the many things they did for me during my college days and after. I feel that they went the extra mile in supporting my move to Washington, D.C., and helping me begin to take care of myself. They were Christian people, helping Christian friends and other people along the way. This is what life is all about!

A New Love

As I mentioned before, many people were coming to Washington to work. One young man started to attend law school at the University of Illinois and was looking for work.

He took a test for a job in J. Edgar Hoover's FBI fingerprinting department in Washington, D.C., and passed it. In 1932, he accepted the job offer and decided to go to Washington as a full-time worker in the fingerprinting department. His plan was to attend Georgetown University Law School to continue working on his law degree. His name was Malcolm Drennan Miller, and one day he would be mine and I his.

Malcolm worked full time in the day and attended school in the evening. After several years, in August 1936, he finished his law work, and graduated from Georgetown University Law School. Then he took the bar exams and passed. He received licenses to practice before the United States Supreme Court and the Supreme Court of Virginia.

At the fingerprinting office, a co-worker by the name of Andy Coleman asked Malcolm what he was going to do with his time now that he had finished his studies. Malcolm's response was that he didn't know because he hadn't had time to think about it. Andy invited him to spend the Labor Day weekend on a trip to the mountains with the Foundry Forge group, and Malcolm accepted this invitation. There were about 50 of us on that Labor Day weekend trip.

There were enough cars that everyone had a ride to the Appalachian Mountains to visit Bear Trail Camp, where we stayed for the three-day weekend. The owners of the camp had a large cabin with a large fireplace where our group activities took place. The men slept in separate cabins, and the women slept upstairs in the larger cabin with the fireplace.

Since this was Malcolm's first time being with the group, and because he was a bit shy, he was standing alone. I noticed this, and I went over to meet him. He was just about the only one on the trip that I didn't know, and I felt he needed a little attention. As it turned out, he loved to hike, and we hiked up to the top of Old Rag Mountain with the group. This was quite a climb. It was the highest point of this area and offered a terrific view. It was while resting at the top that we started enjoying each other's company.

On a log at Bear Trail.

There were many activities that weekend, lots of good food, singing, and visiting around the fireplace. A few brave souls even took a dip into the mountain stream of cold running water near the cabin. Malcolm was one of the brave souls. At Bear Trail, we also would sit around the fireplace, roast marshmallows, and make s'mores, which were so good. After coming back from the weekend, where everyone had a wonderful time, my friendship with Malcolm continued to grow.

Before very long, we were dating. Often, we would walk from the church up Connecticut Avenue to Lamont Street, or we would walk to the church. Apparently my roommate felt a little neglected because I was too busy spending my time with Drennan—that was what he asked me to call him. His father's name was Malcolm Foote Miller, so his family called him by his middle name, Drennan. We were spending all of our spare time together. I began to feel as though Mary were keeping something from me during this time, as though there was a secret being held among her and a few other friends. I felt excluded from her activities, but she didn't tell me what it was about until later.

The Proposal

Malcolm Drennan Miller hiking with me on Labor Day weekend, 1936.

My little romance with Drennan developed quickly. Before I knew it, he was asking me to marry him. This happened one Sunday evening after walking home from church together. After strolling along Connecticut Avenue and 16th Street to Lamont Street, I thought he was probably tired, and then we would finish the evening up by saying goodbye because he still had further to walk to get home. But instead of saying goodbye, while we were standing on the front porch, he stood in front of me, put his arms around me and said, "I love you. Will you marry me?" I was flabbergasted and hardly knew what to do or say. He hugged me tight and kissed me. He was so serious that I felt he was pressing me for an answer.

My heart wanted to say yes, but I wasn't entirely ready. I knew that he was a loving and intelligent person with a Christian upbringing: very honest, very respectful, non-smoking, and non-drinking. My thoughts were that he had all of the positive qualities to be an ideal husband. What more could I ask in such a special friend? I finally said, "Yes, but we must wait for a year."

He was very serious about the engagement because without consulting me in any way, he bought a diamond engagement ring and gave it to me, which I found very exciting. I accepted the ring.

I was warned by a coworker in the Home Service department that I must not let my supervisor know or I would lose my job. For almost a year, I wore my diamond pinned to my bra so Miss Sheldon would not know I was engaged to be married. Miss Sheldon didn't allow any married women in her department, for she, herself was unmarried. Can you imagine having a diamond ring and not being able to wear it?

I eventually pressed my roommate for an explanation for her secretive behavior. She finally told me that there was a certain group of friends that excluded me because I had a boyfriend and was recently engaged. These women were all single and were jealous of me. Within a year, many of the singles in that exclusive group were all either engaged or married.

Sleuthing

About the time that I was dating Drennan, seeing him every few days, my brother Arthur, not knowing about my developing friendship with Drennan, wrote me a letter. He was a pastor of a church in Wisconsin. He was inviting me to come visit him and his family. He also thought I might like to meet a young man attending his church. He was concerned for my welfare, as usual. I wrote Arthur a letter explaining that I wasn't particularly interested right now because I felt that Drennan was a wonderful person. I also wasn't ready to leave Washington to go anywhere else just yet. I told him that Drennan had graduated from Grinnell College and was a lawyer.

Unbeknownst to me, Arthur contacted Grinnell College, where Drennan got his first degree. He wanted to investigate the man who was dating me. After receiving a letter from the president of the college, he said nothing further about my visit to Wisconsin. I didn't know about this letter until it was sent to me by one of Arthur's children after he died. I found it amusing that my brother was still looking after his little "sis."

All throughout my earlier life, I had entertained thoughts of becoming a missionary; a dream I'd had since my teenage years. But all these ideas were put on the backburner. Many other things were happening. This idea was set aside during my college years. After college I received an offer to teach home economics in Bolivia. I often relied on Arthur for advice. He felt I wasn't quite experienced enough for such a responsibility. Looking back at my high school experience, I wasn't the best student in French, so how could I manage in that country learning an entirely different language, Spanish, and be teaching at the same time? My missionary dreams soon faded as I started to plan our wedding. I thought, "God must have a different plan for me right now."

Drennan's Family

Now it is important that I give a few details about my future husband's family. Malcolm Drennan Miller was born on May 26, 1909, in Waverly, Illinois. He was the firstborn child of Malcolm Foote Miller and Ethel Pease Miller. His father was a pastor for the Congregational church. His mother was a skilled organist and pianist in the churches her husband served. Drennan was the only son among four children. His sisters

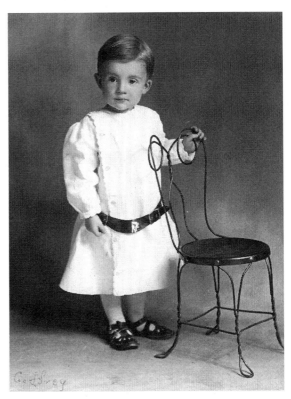

Malcolm Drennan Miller at age 2.

Ruth, Mary, and Esther, were all given Biblical names.

Drennan played the trombone. Ruth and Esther could both play the piano and sing; I don't know what Mary played, if any-

*The Millers, from left: Mary, Malcolm Drennan, their mother
Ethel Pease Miller, father Malcolm Foote Miller, and sisters
Esther and Ruth.*

thing. Their aunt on their father's side, Winifred Miller, was a
very important member of the family. She lived in an old, red
brick house in Abingdon, Illinois. The homestead was considered a landmark in that area but has since been razed. Her
father was a doctor in the town. I still have his crucible on my
kitchen counter. He used it to mix medicines for his patients.

During his teenage years, Drennan was a bit of a loner.
He preferred to read rather than play with the sisters. He had
the reputation as an avid reader and spent the bulk of his time
reading every book in the town library.

Drennan always spoke very highly of his father and his
mother. I remember him saying that "his father preached" way
ahead of the times. When he preached on a subject such as
race relations, he would be asked to leave the church. Why?
Because he was preaching that all people are equal in the sight
of God or something to that effect. As a result, his father would
have to find another church to serve.

Malcolm Foote Miller and Ethel Pease Miller.

Drennan's mother was a tremendous help to his father in serving in the church, with her music helping him spiritually guide the members of the congregation. While she played the church organ during services, Drennan would sit behind it, hand-cranking its fan in order to pump air through the organ. As an interesting aside, he would often read while cranking the organ.

During Drennan's teenage years, his mother, Ethel, was sick with tuberculosis and needed complete rest. Drennan said that he would do the cooking if his sisters would clean up afterwards. So the family managed during this difficult period in their lives.

I was sorry that I didn't get to meet and spend some time with Drennan's family before the wedding weekend. People did very little traveling during the Depression days. Later in life, we saw more of each other than before we were married.

Around the time I was working and getting more acquainted with Drennan, there were still a number of people moving to Washington to work for the government. Norma

Malcolm Drennan Miller's senior portrait.

Small and Herman Miller (no relation) were friends and schoolmates from Evansville, Indiana, who also moved to the Washington area, along with Norma's parents. As I recall, they lived on E Street not too far from the Dodge Hotel. I don't exactly know when Norma and Herman got married, but Drennan and I were soon engaged and we all eventually became good friends.

During the short year that Drennan and I were engaged, we discussed our hopes and expectations as we developed our life together—how many children we hoped to have; where we would plan to live; how we would handle our money; and many other things of interest. Since he was a lawyer, I respected his ideas of what needed to be done before getting the marriage license. Drennan took care of these details. We agreed that we'd never spend money we didn't have. This meant that we'd save money and then buy. I kept the books all our married life (I liked math). When we got married, Drennan was working for the government, and his income was $198 a month.

The Wedding

The first thing we decided was that the wedding would take place in my hometown of Evansville, Indiana, in the little red church I attended as a little girl. The idea was that Drennan's parents and three sisters would have a shorter distance to travel to attend the wedding since they lived in Illinois. There was a carload of friends who drove from Washington to attend the wedding. Some of them had friends in Kansas; they came to our wedding on the way to their destinations to visit their relatives and friends. Fortunately, most of my family lived in Evansville so it was convenient for them to attend.

The next decision was to set a wedding date. We came up with a tentative date of August 26, 1937, one week less than a year from the date we first met. We chose this date because my ring had 12 diamond chips and one larger diamond, making 13 diamonds total. There were two of us getting married, so we doubled 13 to make 26. The date 26 on the August calendar fell on a Saturday, which seemed to be a perfect day for a wedding.

We also consulted Arthur about the wedding date, since we wanted him to officiate at the ceremony.

Instead of giving you a lot of detail, I will summarize the plans for the wedding day weekend. We were planning a very simple wedding for family and friends in Evansville. Drennan's family came the day before the wedding, and we rented some space at a local motel for them to stay. Since Drennan's sisters were musically inclined, I let them pick some of the music for the ceremony. I also asked Esther to play the piano and Ruth to sing. Drennan had his father, a Congregational pastor, be his best man.

I decided to have Norma Miller be my maid of honor. She had moved to Washington, as you recall, and was my closest friend among the young people at the church. She agreed to return to Evansville, Indiana, to participate in the ceremony. Her mother made her dress.

During the year that we were making plans and getting ready for the wedding, I made my own wedding dress. Norma's mother, Mrs. Small, let me use her sewing machine. I stitched a fitted floor-length, empire-waist, satin, sleeveless dress with a full-flowing skirt. The outer layer was made of beautiful French lace. It was also a full-length dress that opened all the way down the front. Eighty-one tiny satin-covered buttons decorated the dress on the front, and from the elbow to the wrist on the sleeves. The lace was only fastened in the front at the waistline. The bridal veil was attached to a satin crown made by braiding some of the satin material used to make the gown. The veil fell to my fingertips.

My wedding portrait.

Remember, this was a simple wedding: Even our wedding invitations were handwritten and mailed to relatives and friends.

In describing all of this planning, I almost forgot to mention the lovely wedding shower that Harriet had for me just a few days before the wedding. This was a linen shower for my aunts and cousins to come to. When the family heard that I was planning to get married, some of my aunts decided to get together and make me a quilt. Only the aunts who were good quilters were allowed to help with this gift. I have treasured this quilt all my life. Others brought linen pillow slips beautifully decorated with hand embroidery. These gifts were easy to pack and take back to Washington with us.

Harriet, my sister-in-law, became very helpful in our wedding plans. She and her sister, Bernice McCutchan, offered to decorate the altar. The altar was a mahogany railing around the pulpit in the front of the church. By the end of August, white Clematis was flourishing and tuberoses were in bloom. They had both planted lots of bulbs the previous spring hoping to have a large supply of flowers to work with. So the church was beautifully decorated for our wedding.

The wedding was planned for an 11 a.m. service with a luncheon scheduled for an hour later. As is the custom, my father gave me away. Everything went as planned, with a wonderful group of relatives and friends present. After the ceremony, we greeted those who attended the service in the lobby of the church.

Our wedding party, from left, Drennan's best man, his father, the Rev. Malcolm Foote Miller; the bridegroom and bride; my father, William Robert Riggs; my bridesmaid and high school friend, Norma Small Miller, who married into a different Miller clan; and my brother, the Rev. William Arthur Riggs, who performed the ceremony.

About 20 members of the immediate families and wedding party gathered at my parents' home for a very simple, private wedding luncheon that Mother and Harriet planned.

The dining room table seated about 14 people and an additional table was set up in the living room to accommodate all the guests. We had fried chicken, German potato salad, fresh green beans, and several relishes, all served family-style. Harriet made a three-tiered, professionally decorated wedding cake and served it with homemade ice cream. After the luncheon we took pictures out in the yard, standing on the sidewalk, in front of the house, and in front of the maple tree.

Everything was nicely done, and the time we all spent together was valuable. At around 3 p.m., Drennan and I were driven to the station, where we took a train back to D.C. My departure outfit was a yellow linen dress with a matching hat and white accessories.

On the train, we traveled in the sleeper and had a private berth. Our time together was very comfortable and private. We stopped in West Virginia for a simple one-night honeymoon before returning to Washington and Arlington, where we planned to live. We also had planned to have a future honeymoon for our first anniversary. As you can probably guess, these were still the days of coming out of the Depression: Very little money was spent on our wedding. The only thing that was purchased was a bouquet for the bride to carry during the wedding ceremony.

Before we left for our wedding in Evansville, Drennan had rented a one-bedroom apartment for us to return to after we were married. This was a new apartment, located near 18th and Veitch Streets, which he rented for $37.50 a month. When we arrived back in town, we had a place where we could put our suitcases and packages down, shut the door, and say we are home.

"May God bless us for many years to come."

Arlington, Virginia

Having established the fact that we were planning to live in Arlington County, Virginia, here is some interesting information about the area. Originally, Arlington County was part of the land that was within the 10-mile square that made up the District of Columbia. More than 50 years later, the

The newlyweds.

federal government saw no need for the land on the Virginia side of the Potomac River, so it gave the land back to Virginia. Part of that land is what now makes up Arlington County.

Before I met Drennan and was still living with the Cleavers, I was going to Foundry Church. Back then, many people considered Arlington County as being "out in the sticks." Most of our newly married Foundry friends were settling in Maryland.

En route to our honeymoon.

When I first moved to the area in 1934, there were about a dozen post offices in Arlington, and the streets were named many different names with no particular order. During the early 1930s, the county reduced its number of post offices and also renamed the streets following the naming pattern of the District of Columbia. In 1935, the streets were named in alphabetical order; one-syllable names were used, followed by two-syllable names, and so forth. The streets running parallel to Arlington Boulevard were numbered streets, North or South. Because of the numbered and alphabetical streets system, it was easier for people to navigate the area.

Arlington has changed considerably since that time. For instance, Rosslyn was known as an undesirable neighborhood in which to live. Before World War II, Arlington was mainly land with a population of about 16,000. Many people became interested in buying land to then sell and generate wealth. A political faction some called the Byrd Machine was in control of the Commonwealth; ordinary people were not paying much attention to the government. But because Arlington was close to the Capitol and downtown Washington, the area eventually developed. The central shopping district was known as Clarendon. You could access Clarendon by trolley from Rosslyn through part of North Arlington.

A lot of government workers found a place to live in the housing development called Colonial Village. Kann's Department store was a landmark in the Virginia Square area, now occupied by the George Mason University Law School, Arlington campus. When World War II broke out, even more people came to work for the government. Along Glebe Road was another housing project similar to Colonial Village known as Buckingham.

Much of this information will be helpful to the reader to understand some of the events that took place during our lives in Arlington County.

Chapter Seven

The Marriage Years

Arriving back in Arlington we settled into our "home" on 18th Street in Colonial Village. Our brand new apartment was on the top floor on the north side of the two-story building. During the years here, we could see part of the construction work of the National Cathedral from our living room and bedroom windows. This apartment had one bedroom, one bathroom, a large living room and a small kitchen. Included in the living room was a double bed that swung out of the closet. It was fastened to hinges on the closet door frame. We could swing it out of the closet, pull the bed down and have a place to sleep. We brought back the linens we received as gifts from the bridal shower and wedding, so we had nice things to use.

All we possessed upon moving in were our clothing, personal items, and linens; we had no real furniture. Our dining room "furniture" consisted of a broken down card table and wooden fruit boxes to sit on. We had two sets of cheap eating utensils and paper plates. A few days after we moved in, members of the Foundry Forge surprised us with a housewarming shower. We received pots, pans, a toaster, and other kitchen equipment.

While on the subject of gifts, there was one special wedding present that I want to mention: *The Boston Cooking School Cook Book*. This was such a wonderful present because at that time I did not have any recipes to go by. *The Boston Cooking School Cook Book* was first published in 1896 and was so popular that it was revised six times before the copy I received. There were nearly two million of the cook books in circulation. I was given the latest edition, and since then it has been revised many times. The author, Fannie Merritt

Farmer, was a pioneer and scholar in the field of cooking, as mentioned in the preface of the cookbook. This book is so important and useful to me that I have used it for 73 years, and it is still the first cookbook I turn to when looking for a recipe.

We had fun "camping" in our apartment until we could afford to purchase some real furniture. In a year's time, we were able to purchase a maple bedroom set. The set consisted of a double bed, side table, chest of drawers, and a dresser.

During the Depression years, it was common for only one person in a household to have a job. Shortly before we left for our wedding, I resigned from my job at the Washington Gas Light Company, and we made a budget according to Drennan's monthly salary of $198. We'd agreed earlier that I would keep the books since I liked math, and that we'd never spend more than we could afford to pay for.

I was very impressed with the fact that my new husband took me to the bank and put my name on his bank account as soon as we returned from the wedding. It was a demonstration of his trust in me. One of the first things we did was plan a budget by listing all of our expenses. These expenses ranged from life insurance premiums, food, rent, clothing, and so forth. The most important thing about every budget is setting aside a percentage for savings. This savings fund is critical for emergencies. Only so much was left for recreation. At the time, all we had left in our budget for recreation was $1.50 a month. We could afford a show for 35 cents each and an ice cream cone for a nickel apiece. All the while we enjoyed one another's company hiking and spending time together.

Twice a week, the milkman would deliver milk by horse and wagon to our doorstep. We'd wash out the used bottles and set them outside on our doorstep for the milkman to take, sterilize and reuse.

As soon as we returned to the Washington area from our wedding, Drennan went back to work because we could not afford any more days off. Some of our wedding gifts were monetary. The first purchase made with these gifts was a sewing machine for me. With the rest of this money, we bought a lovely mahogany desk and a chair, which I still enjoy using today.

I kept busy during the first few months by writing thank you notes, corresponding with family and friends, and meeting new friends in the neighborhood.

One of our first portraits.

I also investigated to see if there was an organization of the American Association of University Women in Arlington County. I discovered that there was no branch here. Several years earlier, I had located the national headquarters in Washington on I Street NW. After having graduated from Purdue and working in the Washington area, I checked the cost of joining. During the Depression years, the annual membership dues were $35, which I couldn't afford.

After about a year and a half, I became pregnant. Now my attention was focused on other things. We began planning for our first baby and purchased a crib to put in our bedroom. William Drennan Miller was born September, 15, 1939. We were so happy—our first-born child was a little healthy boy with curly red hair. This was the time when women were kept in the hospital for two weeks; the staff gave instructions on how to care for a newborn, and they felt this time of rest was good for the mother's womb.

The Foundry young people's group gave us a baby shower. Most of William's early years, as a baby and a toddler, were spent in Colonial Village. We would walk to a playground, where the other children were playing. During this time, Drennan's salary was increasing, and our budget was changed to meet the needs of our family. Over time, we had added a few pieces of used furniture to our collection, so we were comfortable in our small apartment.

We still attended the Foundry Church, where there were a lot of young couples getting married. Many of these couples moved their homes to Maryland. We could not understand this practice because Arlington was so close to the government buildings where many of them were working. Our apartment was within walking distance to the trolley in Rosslyn, which went down Pennsylvania Avenue to the government buildings.

Quite a number of us Depression-era couples decided to keep in touch, particularly the women. We organized a group with the long-debated name of "The 30-40 Group" in reference to the time period in which we all met. As I write this book, there are only two of us left from that original large group. Her name is Alice Vaeth and she is 97 years old. We now keep in touch mainly by telephone but recently had a delightful reunion over lunch at her retirement home in Potomac, Maryland.

The 30-40 Group shared a lot of activities together. One member of the group bought land in Beverly Beach, near Mayo, Maryland. Herman Miller and his father-in-law built a house on the land. We'd often have picnics of covered dishes with a dessert of ripe watermelon in their yard after we went swimming. We'd spend the time chatting and watching the children play on the shallow beach along the clear water of the Chesapeake Bay.

In 1940, we were expecting another baby, so we planned to move into a house. In May, we moved into a small bungalow on Quintana Street, which Drennan had rented with the option to buy. This bungalow had a living room, two bedrooms, a bathroom, a small dining room and kitchen with a porch all on the same level. Our house on Quintana Street, off of Washington Boulevard, was in a wonderful quiet neighborhood perfect for raising a family.

The living room was across part of the front of the house and had a vaulted ceiling that reached 15 feet to the center beam. At the end of the living room was a fireplace alongside a door leading to the screened-in porch. Behind the living room was a small dining room, as well as a kitchen. As we entered the front door, there were steps leading to the second floor. The bedrooms were on the right side of the house. The two bedrooms, one bathroom, and a hallway were entered from the living room.

The hallway had a door to each room, a closet, and a door leading to the basement. Since the house was built on a slope, the back of the house was at ground level with the garage under the bedrooms. This house was a very comfortable, livable house, and we stayed here for 18 years.

Our house on North Quintana Street.

On Washington Boulevard there was a bus route that traveled through Arlington to take us where we needed to go. Eventually, the time finally came when we'd saved up enough money to purchase a second-hand car for $375. This was particularly helpful for getting around town, going to the beach, and taking care of important errands like buying groceries.

At one point, Drennan said to me, "Now I am not going to be your taxicab and take you every place you want to go." My reply was, "Does that mean I have the freedom to go to meetings and things whenever I want to without you?" He said yes and I agreed to be moderate in my personal activities. We were giving each other freedom to do our "own thing." This gave me the freedom to make my own choices regarding my social activities. We agreed that he would watch over the sleeping children during the evenings while I attended my meetings.

Drennan also had the freedom to pursue his own activities, such as attending his Photography Club meetings. This club was focused on artistic photography. Because of the artistry of the group's photographs, the Smithsonian's National Museum of Natural History on Constitution Avenue exhibited their work for a couple of months.

A lot of our time was spent at home developing his photographs at night in the basement. Much equipment was needed for this process: trays, bottles of chemicals for development, thermometers and water. It was always fun to see the images "magically" appear on the photo paper.

About the same time, we started going to Clarendon Methodist Church. We had visited there several times after William was born. It was fortunate that we had moved to a house, even though we lost the pregnancy.

There was a group of women at the church who were regularly having lunch together, and they invited me to come. Friendships began to develop.

All of these women belonged to the Philathea Sunday School Class, so I joined. One of the women, Edith Upperco, soon became my mentor, and a special friend for the rest of her life.

After the December 7, 1941, Japanese attack on Pearl Harbor, the United States entered World War II, and there were many changes taking place. Many things were rationed, such as gas, sugar, and meat. All construction was postponed. Before we moved to the rented house, we had purchased a plot of land with the intention of building a house in North Arlington. The period of building was postponed, so we proceeded to purchase the house we were renting on Quintana Street. We borrowed $6,500 from my mother, which she was glad to loan us, because we promised to pay her back with a little more interest than she would get at the bank. The $6,500 was the total cost of the house. Since the house was now in our name, Drennan could start remodeling the space on the second floor, above the bedrooms. We still had storage space above the dining room and kitchen area, which we called the attic.

Malcolm, Margaret and Winifred

Since we both agreed that we wanted several children in our family, we were happy to discover that I was pregnant again. Although it was almost spring, the day I went into the hospital to give birth was wintry cold, with snow and ice on the ground. Malcolm Robert Miller was born on March 21, 1943. He was our miracle baby. The doctor said, "His birth was difficult—one in a thousand." However, the doctor was able to bring us through okay. When it was time for us to go home from our stay in the hospital, it was a beautiful sunny day and spring flowers were in bloom. It was quite a change of scenery for me because the window in my room had looked out on a brick wall!

Fifteen months later, we were blessed with another baby. Margaret Ann Miller was born June 17, 1944. My mother came each time I gave birth, which was a blessing because she could help me with the other children. Drennan was with me at the hospital that night until 10:00. He decided that he might as well go home because he had a big day coming up at the office. But before he got home, Margaret had arrived and we were both doing fine.

We now had three beautiful, healthy children. They

were all growing nicely and progressing as normal children. I would put them in the car and take Drennan to work so we could have the car to use during the day. Then we would pick him up after work. The children loved to ride in the car.

William, baby Margaret Ann, and little Malcolm joined us for an early family portrait.

To give you an idea of how busy our days were, I will tell you about one day that I shall never forget. I took Drennan to work in the morning and drove on to the farmers market in northeast Washington, where I bought a bushel of June apples. The day before, I had purchased glass canning jars and put them in the oven to sterilize them. While the children were playing in the backyard, I cut and cored the apples and cooked them for a short period of time. I then put the cooked apples through a sieve before placing them in a kettle, seasoning, and heating them and putting them into the sterilized jars. The applesauce was all in the jars by four o'clock, which was about the time to go back to D.C. to pick up Drennan. So, we all got in the car and had a nice ride to pick up "Daddy."

Many weekends, Drennan was very helpful around the house. He would go into the kitchen and make a big pot of soup, especially if we were planning to take the children to the zoo on Sunday afternoon. They loved to go to the zoo to watch the different animals. When we first moved to Quintana Street, we planted an apple tree and a cherry tree. Neither of the trees produced enough fruit for canning, but we did have cherries for pies, and apples to eat.

During the early '40s, a lot was going on in our neighborhood. A family on one side of our home had adopted five children over a period of time. The family on the other side had four boys. Within three houses we had 12 children. Being that our house was in the middle and we had a nice-sized backyard, I suggested to the children to play in our yard. Drennan had built a big swing set out of 2 x 4s. There were three swings and the center one was for the younger children. It had a small child's seat arrangement with a bar across the front so they would not fall out.

As the children grew, it was changed to a regular seat. The kids had a lot of fun swinging. Drennan also built a big sandbox under the cedar tree. With plenty of sand and a little water, they built lots of things in the sand. While they were playing, I was in the kitchen cooking, and I could watch what was going on in the yard. When it was time for them to quit playing in the sandbox, they could take the hose, which was attached to the faucet on the back of the house, and wash off the sand.

In the years prior to public schooling, we helped to organize a kindergarten and preschool for our young children. This was called the Overlee Kindergarten. Another activity taking place in the community was a series of meetings for the planning of a local swimming pool for the families and children to enjoy. Drennan attended these meetings because of his experience as a lifeguard, which made him helpful in planning this project. Our goal was to help produce facilities in the community that would benefit everyone. Families in the community worked together and found land to buy, suitable for having a pool constructed. There was a house on the land purchased for the Overlee Knolls swimming pool. This house served as a community center where members could socialize and enjoy card games and other activities.

Everything seemed to be going along so well until the winter of 1945. I was still nursing Margaret when our oldest child, William, who was 5, became very ill with scarlet fever. It was still war time and there weren't many nurses available. My mother came from Indiana to help take care of William and keep him away from the other children so that they didn't get ill. William became so ill that he died on February 1, 1945. It was Mother who was with him when he died, and she told me that before he died, he raised his arms toward Heaven, and then he dropped down on the bed and was gone. So, I believe God took him home!

At the time, Drennan was in California on a business trip. Our family rarely made telephone calls in those days, so I had to wait until he returned home the next day to tell him that our first-born, William, was gone. This was the saddest time of our life. I think Drennan always felt that if he had been home that perhaps something could have been done to save his son.

Since we were quarantined, no one could enter or leave the house. A little coffin was brought into our living room by the funeral home, and William was placed inside. At this time, we bought a burial plot at the Columbia Gardens cemetery in Arlington. A small ceremony was held at Columbia Gardens Cemetery Chapel located in the heart of Arlington near Arlington Boulevard and Glebe Road. The doctor told us that had he lived, William would have been an invalid for the rest of his life.

Our friends, neighbors, and family surrounded us with love and sympathy. Our little William was a lover of books during his earthly years. Many financial donations were made in his memory, and we used the money to start a Children's Memorial library at Clarendon United Methodist Church. The Children's Memorial library is still a part of the Helter Church Library, which was established in our church much later.

Our three children, Margaret, Winifred and Malcolm, in 1947.

A few months after William died, I read that penicillin was now available to the public. It had been discovered in the 1920s and had taken that long to be approved for use by the general public. I have always felt that it probably would have saved him.

During our period of grieving, we tried to look toward the future. While William Drennan would always be in our hearts, Drennan and I agreed that another child would be welcome. Malcolm and Margaret were growing and we, as a family, were moving on with our usual activities. Winifred Evelyn Miller was born on March 9, 1946, around the time Drennan and I started to get involved in working for better schools in Arlington County.

In the meantime, Drennan had resigned from his government job and opened his own law office on Vermont Avenue close to K Street NW, in the District of Columbia. He had worked for the Interstate Commerce Commission and the Office of Price Administration on cases related to the rates charged for transporting merchandise. In his private practice, he specialized in transportation rate cases. He was also a trial lawyer for the Post Office Department in railway mail pay cases. He decided to run his law office without the help of a secretary. He typed his own briefs, duplicated them, and we assembled them around the dining room table in the evenings.

Clarendon Methodist Church

The Clarendon church building had been finished and dedicated in May of 1941. This was a blessing because war was declared in December of that year, when all building was postponed.

The builders were dedicated Christians who were devoted to the construction of the church. The stained-glass windows on the left side of the sanctuary (facing the altar), depicted the stories of the Old Testament, from front to back. The windows on the other side of the sanctuary, leading towards the front, tell the stories of events from the New Testament ending with the crucifixion of Jesus. The sanctuary is a wonderful place to worship and pray. Many people wished to have their wedding there and still do to this day because it is such a beautiful sanctuary.

Clarendon United Methodist Church.

Clarendon has always been a community church reaching out to its neighbors. Very early in the life of the church, a kindergarten was organized for the children to be trained and schooled. The Schick pipe organ was another outstanding feature of the church; it was financed by donations and installed in 1967. I remember Mr. Wigent being the first organist of the Schick organ; due to health reasons he had to resign. Dr. Reilly Lewis became our organist in 1971. We recently celebrated his 40th anniversary as the organist at our church.

Nan Manning and her husband were great leaders in our church. He owned many plots of land and an oil station in Clarendon, and was helpful in locating the land where the church was built. Many young couples were joining the church, so Nan and I decided to get together a group of university women in the area and started forming monthly meetings. We were both having our children and had many interests in common. Our group was growing in size, and when gas was rationed because of the war, we started meeting in two groups: one for North Arlington, and one for South Arlington. In 1944, the groups came together to organize an official branch of the American Association of University Women, known as AAUW.

Son William Drennan Miller and the bookplate honoring his memory.

CHILDREN'S LIBRARY

This Book

in

Memory of

WILLIAM

DRENNAN

MILLER

Clarendon Methodist Church

Nan and I also organized a child study group, which included other mothers from the community. We had people trained in raising children to come and speak at our meetings. We had a chance to ask questions and learn much about normal growth in toddlers and how to take care of them.

The church was growing by leaps and bounds. I was still attending the Philathea class, but all they were doing, before and after class, was talking about their teenaged children. Marion Elliot and I felt the need to organize a young mother's Sunday school class. We both agreed that we would need some help to do this, and asked Edith Upperco if she would help us. After the three of us talked, we prayed about it, and she said she would, if she could ask Elizabeth Brazil to help. After a little bit more red tape, we put a notice in the church bulletin inviting mothers of young children to join us. During the first year, the class had more than 50 members, so we moved from the original meeting room to the church balcony. We also had the idea of bringing food to the social hall to enjoy after the worship service to encourage communication among the members of the church, a practice that continues today.

We called ourselves the Fidelis Sunday school class. Right now there are about eight of us still living, half of whom reside in nursing homes. When the class was organized in 1944, the members chose the name, "Fidelis" because it means faithful. This prayer was included in the front of our membership book:

"Give me the FAITH that asks not 'Why?'
I shall know God's plan by and by.
Give me the FAITH that looks at pain
And says: 'Twill all be right again.'
Give me the FAITH that clasps God's hand,
When things are hard to understand.
Give me the FAITH to bow my head
Trustingly, waiting to be led.
Give me the FAITH to face my life
With all its pain and wrong and strife.
And then with the day's setting sun
I'll close my eyes when life is done.
My soul will go without a care
Knowing that God is waiting there."

We closed our weekly classes with this benediction:

"A charge to keep I have
Give me thy Power Divine
May all my loved ones feel Thee near,
And grace and strength be mine."

After several years, our class numbered 94 members and was a very active group in the life of the church. There is a book on the history of the church written in 1996 by Phyllis Johnson, who acknowledges our contribution to the fellowship time in the social hall.

With three children in tow, it was only natural that I wanted to learn more about childrearing. I eventually developed an interest in the county's school system. Many other young couples with children shared such an interest. We later discovered that the schools were in poor condition. In the mid-1940s, Drennan and I became very involved in working for good schools in the county. Our struggle is detailed in the following chapter.

Chapter Eight

Working for Better Schools

T he decade of the '40s was an exciting and interesting time to be involved in the political situation in Arlington County.

Many young couples were moving into this area to work for the federal government, which was trying to help the country come out of the Great Depression. Then, many others moved into the area during World War II. This population influx across the Potomac from Washington, D.C., came from all areas of the country. Many of these newcomers were families concerned with the needs of their children, especially education.

An article written by Dr. Oscar LeBeau appeared in one of the Washington newspapers announcing a meeting for people who were interested in the establishment of a kindergarten class for their children. The meeting was to take place at the Buckingham residential community center. This caught the attention of many young parents and parents-to-be. Since we had very young children, I told Drennan that I wanted to attend the meeting because we were, of course, very interested in the welfare of our children.

About 50 people came to the first meeting. The more we discussed the condition of the schools, the more we realized it was necessary to get organized to improve the situation. This strong interest in academic affairs led to the development of the Citizens Committee for School Improvement (CCSI). Dr. LeBeau assumed the responsibility of leading this committee.

*Joseph Wheeler, left, and Malcolm Drennan Miller, right, with
Oscar LeBeau, who led the fight for better schools in Arlington.
They were photographed for a 1950 Saturday Evening Post article
about the drive for an elected school board.*

We began trying to work with the local school board to
make changes. At the time, Virginia was under the influence
of a Democratic organization some called the Byrd political
machine. Harry F. Byrd Sr. had risen to the position of U.S.
Senator. Because of his family connections, he was able to
have power, prestige, and influence over many things in Virginia. He also strongly adhered to a "pay-as-you-go" type of
government: Education was very low on his priority list.

Arlington County's school board was chosen like this:
The governor appointed the Circuit Court judge who in turn
appointed an electoral board, which then appointed a local
school board. It's obvious that it made the school board very

far removed from the citizens of the community.

In addition, Virginia was caught up in the plantation owner idea of education: The custom was for plantation owners to have private tutors for their children. Those who had money could send their children to private schools, which were often started by churches. Public schools were first started in Virginia in 1870 and were considered in the realm of charity for poor families. In other parts of the country, public schools had existed for two centuries.

The Byrd Machine and the way the school board was appointed had stymied efforts of parents to improve public education in Arlington. Some parents drove their children to the better, tuition-free schools in the District; those who could afford it sent their children to private schools.

After the CCSI was organized, a small group of us soon realized that we would need an updated voters' list, so we proceeded to do something about it. To finance it, eight of us decided to put $50 each into a fund: Joe and Shirley Wheeler, O.B. Allen, Virginia Thatcher, Joe and Luella Ingram, my husband and myself. The group decided that I would be chairperson of this project.

I knew that I could do this and still be at home with the children. I had been attending CCSI meetings and recognized that it needed a lawyer. I told Drennan he should help the group working for better schools, so Drennan began to attend the CCSI meetings.

Voter Lists for Mobilization

I asked the CCSI for volunteers and organized them to create a list of voters. We took turns going into the county courthouse office to copy all the names from the official voters' list. We wrote voter names and addresses on 3 x 5 index cards, alphabetized and organized them by precinct, and put them in a shoebox. We also developed a network of chairpersons for every precinct. We asked these chairpersons to call on every address listed on their cards to verify the information.

Each 3 x 5 card that could not be verified, or if information had changed due to moving or death, was reported to the courthouse registrar who kept the official voters' list. Each chairperson gathered a group of workers who were willing to work in any way to get good schools.

We made stencils with the correct information for every contacted name and address. Stencils for the Elliot Addressograph system were small rectangular frames with a window of film in the center designed for typing an address. The stencils were made by placing this frame into an old-fashioned typewriter. When each letter was pushed, the hammer would cut that letter into the film and create the stencils. This way, ink could pass through the cut stencil. These were used to address the literature to be mailed to the county voters.

We bought a large file cabinet in which to keep our alphabetized stencils so that the list could be easily updated and used to address literature for mailing. Drennan and I kept this file cabinet in the basement of our home. I spent most of my time on the phone updating the names in every precinct.

Having an up-to-date list of voters was the basis of our strenuous activities for the CCSI. A voters' list is only as valuable as its accuracy and reliability. Our efforts to keep it current guaranteed an organized method of informing the voters through our distribution of literature regarding what we were doing to improve the school system.

While I was working on the voters' list, Drennan was very active in attending the CCSI meetings. We already knew that there were only half-day sessions for first- and second-graders and there was no such thing as kindergarten. We had nothing in the schools that we think of as necessary today in 2012: no libraries, no cafeterias, no gyms.

There weren't even enough school buildings to house the population that was moving to this area. And, the buildings that did exist were poorly lit and equipped. In addition to electric light bulbs hanging from the ceilings in run-down buildings, there were many things that needed to be improved.

We wanted to take care of these things, but always found that the budget for education would not support our ideas. No one was interested in having their taxes go up. Many people in the area who held a lot of real estate didn't have children in the public school system, and they didn't want to pay for improvement.

In our efforts to work for better schools, a group attended a meeting where the school board was discussing the budget. Dr. LeBeau was trying to get the board to put more money into schools, and the leadership told him that the budget did not include an increase for the schools. He asked, "Well, how do we get more money for the schools?"

They very reluctantly told him that he needed to get 1,000 voters' signatures on a petition to propose this as a bond issue. Since LeBeau was serious about getting money to spend on the schools, he took several sheets of paper and started collecting signatures at that meeting.

Since they needed names on the petition, there was already an organized way to get them: from people who were checking the accuracy of the voters' list. This gave each precinct chairperson excellent information to collect signatures for the proposed bond issue.

In a very short time, 5,000 names were collected! We took this good news to the school board, which soon realized the significance of getting a bond issue on the next scheduled election in November. The board threw this information and hard work into a drawer and forgot about it. The school board was not trying to work with us at all.

The CCSI continued to meet to try to figure out things members could do to keep working for good schools. And then at one meeting, as the Saturday Evening Post later put it, a smart young lawyer had the brilliant idea of changing the method of choosing the school board! The smart young lawyer was my husband, who immediately got busy writing a simple bill to take to the legislature in Richmond. The bill would amend the 1930 law that established Arlington's county manager form of government to permit an elected, instead of an appointed, school board.

After the meeting that evening, Drennan came home at 1:30 a.m. I was still up doing housework, and he asked me, "Do you have a clean white shirt for me to wear?"

"Yes," I answered, "but why at this time in the morning?"

He explained that he and a group were going to Richmond to introduce a bill they'd been working on that evening. They wanted to be in Richmond in time to have breakfast at 6 a.m. with the local representatives of Arlington County. The drive would take about four hours.

It was so important to get the bill there because the legislature was in special session for two weeks. There, the group asked our representatives to introduce the bill, which would allow an election in Arlington County to see if the voters wanted an elected school board.

The Arlington delegation thanked the CCSI people for their interest in government and agreed to introduce the bill to both the House and Senate. But they said they didn't think it stood a chance of passage. Drennan replied, "'We'll be here every day until this bill is passed."

The House passed the measure, but it languished in a Senate committee. As the Senate was in recess, waiting on the last day of the session for the House to finish its work, the CCSI members who had taken turns driving to Richmond every day for two weeks realized there was little time to salvage their effort. They were invited onto the Senate floor to chat with the members who were there.

One of the CCSI women, using a drawl, spoke up, saying that since the Senate wasn't doing anything, why not bring the CCSI's bill out of committee. She was told that was never done, but she reportedly replied, "Why don't you try?" The senator took that as a dare, and the bill was brought out of committee. Challenged by another CCSI woman to bring the bill to a vote, the senators finally agreed to call the Senate back into session and voted to approve the bill.

When Drennan and his cohorts returned triumphant from Richmond, they filled us in on all of the details of how the bill finally was passed, as I've just described.

The CCSI campaign took the entire two weeks of the special session. It took a considerable amount of volunteering by the Arlingtonians who went to Richmond daily to lobby for the bill. Because so many Arlingtonians worked for the federal government, they were subject to the restrictions of the Hatch Act, which prohibited them from being involved in political parties. Therefore, CCSI members had to work as independent citizens.

When the governor signed the bill, the CCSI had accomplished its goal for the special session.

Now it could be put to a vote in Arlington. The issue was, "Did Arlington County want an elected school board?" The vote was overwhelmingly for an elected board.

On the same May 1947 ballot, the appointed board had placed questions about $6 million in bond issues to fund school improvements, apparently thinking that the large amount would not pass. The calculation was correct, because voters only agreed to one of the four bond issues: $1,776,000 to expand elementary school facilities. At least any new elected board would have some money to work with, though it was not enough.

What Next?

We had not thought through how this transition to an elected board would occur. None of the CCSI members who campaigned for the elected board was particularly interested in running. Our goal had been to have the privilege of electing our own school board. Now that we had that right, the real work began in earnest of getting qualified, electable candidates on the ballot. Planning the process for electing the school board was the next important step.

In addition to leaders in the community with a willingness and desire to run, there was a strong need for people with backgrounds in building, education, and other relevant fields. Planning for the total number of members of an elected school board called for examining other schools in districts that had elected school boards. The CCSI solicited ideas from those with a background in government and education. It was also important to the CCSI to have a balanced school board: The ideal members would have knowledge or experience in the different aspects of education so that they could work together to develop a good school system. To help meet that need, the leaders conducted a number of interviews to find interested county citizens to represent our group.

First they surveyed communities with elected school boards for advice on what steps to take. As a result of this research, it was decided that they would sponsor a nominating convention. Since the CCSI was also very interested in making this not just an organizational matter, but a county affair, they invited other groups to participate. Many other Arlington County organizations responded to the invitation.

After planning the details for this public nominating convention and soliciting names for nominees, a date for the convention was set for August. The other groups brought their own slate of possible candidates to this convention. By that time, the CCSI had five people in mind and asked them to attend. These people were outstanding citizens of the county and were willing to run if selected.

Image from March of Time, courtesy Time Inc.
Son Malcolm tacks up a handbill for the school board election.

At the convention, all nominees could refuse to run if they so chose. The five candidates who received the highest number of votes from this convention were to be added to the ballot for the official school board election in November. Of the 15 who accepted nominations that night, the five who received the most votes were the ones suggested by CCSI.

The final school board ballot included four members of the old school board, three interested citizens, and the five candidates nominated by the CCSI. This made a total of 12 candidates on the ballot for the five seats on the board.

After the candidates list was settled, the next step was to prepare for the November election. The CCSI went into high gear. As its membership rose to 1,400, the excitement of working toward the goal increased. With the help of having an accurate voters' list, every household was visited and several mailings of literature were sent and telephone calls were made in support of our candidates. They were Elizabeth P. Campbell, the former dean of a women's college; O. Glenn Stahl, an educator, orator and my first cousin, who was deputy director of personnel for the Federal Security Agency; Curtis E. Tuthill, a professor at George Washington University; Colin C. MacPherson, a local builder, and Barnard Joy, who worked for the U.S. Department of Agriculture.

CCSI volunteers contacted every registered voter in every precinct personally. Along with informing the citizens, we strove to educate and encourage unregistered persons to register to vote so that they too could get involved in the welfare of their children's schools and education. The campaign was a success, and we were now able to proceed with assisting the elected school board in improving the county's school system.

This whole process of citizens getting together and working for a goal so impressed people in New York that they sent a movie company to the area to document our work. The March of Time film was called "The Fight for Better Schools." This film was shown throughout the country as an example of how citizens could impact their communities by working together for a common goal. I still have a copy of the film.

After the CCSI slate of candidates was elected to the school board, the new board members began meeting and visiting schools in the area to examine what needed to be improved. They were appalled at their observations.

Many things had to be considered in order to develop a plan of action.

Despite ongoing financial oppression from the Byrd Machine, it was decided that the first school to be built would be Stratford Junior High School. Before any building actually started, many people were involved in the planning process. One of the first tasks was to appoint people to 14 committees for every aspect of public education, including subjects to be taught. I was appointed to the Home Economics Committee. The purpose of these committees was to study the needs in their particular area and to feed this information for the school board to use to help make decisions. This was a wonderful technique to use because it kept many people working on the ideas of school improvement. To this day, there are still citizen committees to advise the Arlington school board.

The CCSI's intense focus was extremely powerful and influential. I learned in recent years that we caused a great deal of disturbance in the political realm of the county. The Machine was not happy with the progress and publicity of the CCSI. Real estate investors were not pleased with the idea of paying more property taxes to cover the cost of improving the school system. As we worked toward approval of an elected school board, we were called communists and foreigners. People spoke about us as if we were criminals coming to the area to take over. Many people, however, recognized that the quality of Arlington County's schools and government are a result of our driven activism in the '40s. Today, Arlington schools rank high among the nation's best public education systems.

A lot of the activity of getting our county an elected school board happened in our basement. Our small group was responsible for updating the voters' list that was used for the Addressograph system. This is where the children got involved. They used to love to help crank the Addressograph machine so that we could get the names on the literature and ready it for mailing. Margaret, our third child, was very interested in how the stencils were placed in the trays alphabetically. She wanted to help, and prior to starting school, this helped her to learn how to alphabetize.

After the main goals of the CCSI for school improvement were reached, there was less of a need for a voters' list to be kept. Rumor had it that another citizen's activist group, known as the Better Government League, was also focused on improving the quality of society by implementing good county government, thus they shared an interest in the voters' list. We informed them that our small group was interested in getting rid of the voters' list, so we sold the voters' list and equipment to this more politically oriented group focused on bettering the county government.

We didn't recoup the original $400 investment or the expenses we had incurred to update the list. But I, personally, was happy to be rid of this responsibility so that I could focus my attention on the needs of our growing family. It was a joy and a privilege to have been part of this community effort. It is the legacy we have left to Arlington County.

Epilogue

In 1959, after Arlington defied Virginia's "Massive Resistance" campaign and integrated the first public school in the Commonwealth, the legislature rescinded permission for an elected school board. Until 1992, the elected Arlington County Board appointed the school board. After that, we once again had the opportunity to elect our school board members.

Chapter Nine

Meeting Life's Challenges

The Family

After the new school board was elected in 1948, I no longer had the responsibility of keeping the voters' list current. I had great joy in focusing more on my children and their activities.

Throughout the years of our political involvement, Drennan and I always made time to enrich our children's lives. I introduced them to a host of activities such as tap dancing, ballet, and acrobatics. The kids, as I mentioned before, loved visiting the zoo at Rock Creek Park to see all of the animals.

At home, they enjoyed the swing set and large sandbox their father built from 2 x 4s! The larger wood made them much bigger and sturdier. The swing set was on one side of the cedar tree and the sandbox on the other.

My husband was a wonderful woodworker who loved to construct. After we moved into the two-bedroom bungalow on Quintana Street, Drennan renovated our second-floor space into a nice bedroom for Malcolm. The room functioned as a playroom and a bedroom, with two double beds that rolled away under the eaves when not in use for sleeping. We transformed them into davenports during the day by placing the pillows on top where they leaned against the paneled walls. In the evenings, when the children were all ready for bed, we would have story time.

In April 1949, our family life changed considerably. Drennan's sister, Ruth (who sang at our wedding), had just given birth to her second son and became ill. Her husband, Robert Allen, asked if we would consider taking care of his two boys while Ruth spent time in the hospital. Bob had his doctorate in bacteriology and was working on getting a medical degree. Because of all that was going on in the Allen household, John and Richard were two little additions to the Miller household. Our youngest child, Winifred, and the Allens' oldest boy, John, were just three months apart in age, so they became our "twins." The newborn boy, Richard, was just three months old when he came to live with us.

I now had five preschool-aged children to take care of, and this was a full-time job. We had them as part of our family for the better part of seven years. During this time, Bob was able to furnish some money to help care for the children. I was then able to hire help to make it a little easier for me to handle the situation. My helper, Virgie, had two school-aged boys of her own, and she was excellent with the children. She really needed the job to help provide for her family.

The five cousins with their grandfather Malcolm Foote Miller, back. In front is Richard Allen; left to right are John Allen, and Winifred, Margaret and Malcolm Miller.

From the left, John, Malcolm, Margaret, Richard and Winifred.

By the fall of 1949, Malcolm was ready to begin first grade at age six. Drennan and I were also involved in working on starting a kindergarten group in a local church, which 5-year-old Margaret and 3-year-old Winifred and John attended. About this time, our son Malcolm wanted a paper route so he could be earning some money. (By the time he was 7, he had a

fairly large route and was thriving under this responsibility.)
There was just one problem. In order for him to be on time for
Sunday School and church on Sunday mornings, he needed
some help. So the girls, Malcolm, John, and I would go in the
car and help deliver the papers, while Drennan stayed behind
with Richard. Then, we would eat breakfast and get ready to
go to church. This system worked well.

Drennan was in private law practice, specializing in
transportation and communication cases related to rate
charges. He was also serving as a delegate to the Arlington
County Civic Federation for the CCSI. In 1950, Drennan was
awarded the Washington *Evening Star* Silver Trophy, which
was quite an honor.

*Malcolm Drennan Miller receives the Evening Star Trophy in
1950.*

Each year, Arlington County chose an outstanding citizen
to receive this award, and his name was engraved on the side
of the cup. Then the recipient kept the cup for a year in his

home to enjoy the honor.

An article published in *The Evening Star* on May 3, 1950, noted that "Malcolm D. Miller, chairman of the Revenues and Expenditures Committee of the Arlington Civic Federation, was named by the federation last night as the winner of *The Evening Star* Trophy awarded annually for outstanding civic work." Drennan was also the representative of the Civic Federation to the metropolitan area meetings. These meetings were conducted to discuss various issues that affected the whole area. In one of the meetings with the metropolitan group, he was the first to mention the need for a rail system for the metropolitan area.

During the next spring, Drennan noticed he could not see very well, and decided to go to an eye doctor. He was diagnosed with a detached retina. This wasn't an unusual problem for people who are very nearsighted, as Drennan was. Since the doctor felt he needed special care, he recommended that he see a retina specialist at Johns Hopkins Hospital in Baltimore. After the doctor examined him, he prescribed that Drennan was to remain flat on his back in a hospital for 30 days. The idea behind this treatment was that gravity would cause the retina to be pulled back into place and reattach to the eye.

As a result of this diagnosis, Drennan immediately checked into the hospital and began treatment. This meant that I would travel back and forth every day to see him. Fortunately, I had Virgie helping me during this time, so she would take care of the children and help me while I was away attending to Drennan. During his hospital stay, I tried to act as his secretary by going to the office and picking up his mail and other work-related documents, but since I wasn't a secretary, as you can imagine, things didn't go very well.

Drennan instructed me on how to inform all of his clients of his current health situation. Fortunately, all of them were able to remain with him through his recovery. The treatment was successful. After Drennan was released from the hospital, he gradually began returning to his former work schedule. During this time, I drove Drennan to and from his law office and had to drive the car very carefully so as not to hit a bump in the road; any sudden jarring could cause further splitting of the retina.

My Career

While Drennan was in the hospital, I thought it was a good idea to put in an application for substitute teaching with the local school board. It wasn't long before I was called, and in early February of 1952 I went to substitute for a home economics teacher who had resigned to move to Kansas with her husband. So the school system was looking for a teacher who was qualified to finish out the year. Since I had graduated from a well-known university with a degree in home economics, I was fully qualified, and they hired me. As it turned out, I applied for a substituting job and ended up teaching for 21 years at the same school!

My first day of substitute teaching was on February 12, 1952; I was to teach home economics in the newly built Stratford Junior High School. As the school administration searched for a teacher, they observed that I was a graduate of Purdue University with good credentials. Being a Purdue graduate in the very subject I was substituting in made me a suitable candidate for the job, and I was offered a permanent position for the remainder of the school year.

When the administration announced that I was to finish out the school year, fellow teachers made a comment that I'd arrived just in time. "In time for what?" I asked. It turned out that if one started to work before February 15, it would be counted as an entire year of teaching.

The teacher I was replacing, Mrs. Mintern, was a pretty young woman who kept her fingernails polished and every hair in place. The students all loved her very much. I went into the job not as a slender, petite woman, but as a less petite, well-proportioned woman; the students, all girls, didn't make it any easier by comparing me to their former teacher. At one point, I pounded my fist on the desk and declared that all talk of Mrs. Mintern was finished. From then on, we all got along quite well because they knew who was in charge.

Part of my job teaching eighth-grade home economics was

136

planning the meals and projects to teach my students cooking and sewing. I began planning and shopping not just for myself and my family, but for my students as well. They were almost through the unit on cooking when I began as their teacher. In addition to learning how to prepare meals, my students learned proper etiquette.

The rest of the year I spent teaching the students how to sew. The girls were given the opportunity to sew an apron or skirt. Since each girl had a sewing kit and had learned the use of the sewing machine in their seventh-grade home economics class, the lessons for the eighth-grade class were more focused on planning and constructing a garment and mastering essential sewing skills. There were lessons on changing thread, testing stitches on scrap fabric, and the safe way to handle a sewing machine. Since craftsmanship and creativity were the primary parts of the final grade, everything from the choice of fabric to color schemes and clothing pattern was carefully planned in the project by each girl. Some girls finished their projects early and would be able to choose another project to work on.

I really enjoyed teaching home economics because the girls felt that they were learning a lot of important life skills. I want to tell about a very rewarding experience I had when one of my former students came to me and said, "Mrs. Miller, I made my dress! You taught me all I need to know." It was a beautiful white graduation dress she'd constructed all by herself. I could sense her love for sewing, and it made me feel great about my short time teaching home economics.

The hardest part about teaching this subject was that I could not take the girls' projects home with me to grade, so I had to spend additional time at school. This was sometimes difficult because I had five children at home, and I couldn't spend as much time with them as I wanted to.

In the spring of 1952, the Commonwealth of Virginia made science a mandatory subject to be taught in eighth grade. Having to put science into the curriculum meant that an existing subject had to go. The home economics course soon became an optional subject for girls to take, if they had room in their schedules. When the principal realized that fewer teachers were needed for home economics, he suggested that I teach math instead. The reason I could teach math was because I took a number of mathematics courses back at Purdue. You'll remember that when I first came to Washington, D.C., and found a job, I'd also applied to teach in the D.C. schools. I was under-qualified because I hadn't taken enough teaching courses in math. It was then that I took correspondence courses to get the necessary subjects in order to be qualified to teach. Because of these requirements, I was just as qualified to teach math as home economics. We never know when we will use the information we're told we need!

While I adored home economics, I was grateful that they asked me to teach math because that was my next love. I hated to make the change, but I soon realized that if I wanted to have a teaching job I would have to do so. As it turned out this switch was a blessing: I could take the students' assignments and tests home with me to grade and correct. I usually did this after we put the children down to sleep. I also used this time to plan the next day's lesson.

Teaching math called for an entirely different approach than teaching home economics. The reason for this was that in math class, the students had to understand every idea as we went along, while in home economics, they could be more independent, creative, and constructive about what they were working on. I eventually adapted to what was required of me. It was a blessing to teach a subject that worked better with the needs of my family.

The Allens

During this time, Drennan's sister, Ruth, was still in the hospital, and I was still taking care of her two boys. It turned out that she had suffered from a chemical imbalance after the birth of her second child. Her mental condition made her unable to take care of her boys for a number of years. Her husband, Bob, made time to come and visit the boys when it was convenient. He was still working, studying to become a doctor, and looking after Ruth's needs. A position at the

National Institutes of Health was waiting for him upon graduation. By 1954, Bob was interning at Johns Hopkins Hospital.

The doctors where Bob was working requested his approval to conduct an experiment on his wife by using a "miracle drug" for her condition. She was given the medication during Thanksgiving weekend and she was out of the hospital by Christmas. Ruth had struggled with her chemical imbalance in hospitals for *six years*. As far as the Allens were concerned, this medicine truly was a miracle drug. The doctor said she must work a year before she and Bob could assume the responsibility of caring for their children. After all, this was a new drug, and they wanted to be sure of its effect over a long period of time. Once out of the hospital, Ruth obtained employment at a library near their home in Baltimore.

A year later, over Thanksgiving weekend, Bob and Ruth were on the way to our house to bring the boys back from a family visit. It was Sunday, November 27, 1955, John's 10th birthday. They stopped for a service in the District at President Eisenhower's church, National Presbyterian Church, which then was on Connecticut Avenue near Dupont Circle. Near the end of the service, Bob wasn't feeling well and got up and went to the back of the church. Shortly someone came to get Ruth. Bob was having a heart attack. They had called an ambulance, but he died on the way to the hospital. Bob was 45.

My memory is not clear on how we handled the shock of that day. I was responsible for the children at home while Drennan was helping Ruth to do what she needed to do. Drennan helped Ruth with all of the funeral arrangements, including the purchase of the graveside plot next to ours at Columbia Gardens where our son William was buried.

Ruth still needed to complete her first year of working after being out of the hospital. In late spring of 1956, she felt that she was ready to take care of her boys. As soon as they were under her care, she moved to Abingdon, Illinois. They went to live for a year in the Miller family home, with Aunt Winifred. Built and inhabited by Drennan's grandfather, this home was a landmark in the town of Abingdon.

Since Winifred Miller was the sister of Drennan's father, Malcolm Foote Miller, she was a special aunt in the family. She was also quite a character and a teacher with 56 years of teaching under her belt. I often told her she should have written a book about her teaching and discipline methods. She lived all her life in the three-level homestead that was built in the 1800's.

Winifred had the reputation of getting hundreds of letters at Christmas time and throughout the year from her former students. In her latter years, she was principal of the school, taught math, fired up the furnace, and took care of all the discipline. She used to tell a story about how she would purposely step on a squeaky board in the hallway so that the children could quiet down before she walked in the room. That way, no one would have to be disciplined for noise or behavior. Her discipline, when warranted, tended to fit the crime. She kept dry bread in her desk drawer that she'd give to chatty students to keep them quiet.

I regret to say that Aunt Winifred expected the children of her nephew to be perfect. If I'd known it at the time I would have stopped it, but I found out years later that when she was visiting us once she washed my daughter Margaret's mouth out with soap for calling her sister "Winnie." This nickname apparently did not sit well with Aunt Winifred. It's one of several memories my daughter has about this otherwise wonderful woman.

Whenever we visited Aunt Winifred's, Margaret and the others enjoyed dressing up in the costumes she had there from school plays. She also had a dumb waiter in her home that the children found fascinating.

One interesting thing happened in the family that I think is worth mentioning: Drennan and I had named our second daughter after Aunt Winifred. As a result, Winifred Evelyn Miller was put in Aunt Winifred's will to inherit a silver service set, as other family members had predicted. Historically, this silver was particularly special because it was originally a gift to George Washington by the silversmith in Alexandria, Virginia, who was an ancestor of the Miller family. Since the Washingtons already had another silver set like it, the silversmith took it back and gave the Washingtons a different gift. So this silver service set has been kept in the family and passed down to this day. As it happened, when Winifred Evelyn got married, she did not care for the inheritance. The plan was to have it appraised, give Winifred the monetary equivalent of its value, and pass on the service set to our older daughter Margaret. Because the girls were not yet ready for it at the time of Aunt Winifred's passing, Drennan and I kept the silver service in our home, and put it to good use for a number of years.

Another family heirloom that came down from Aunt Winifred's estate was an English mahogany table, constructed in England and made with wooden hinges. Since Malcolm Drennan Miller could trace his ancestry to the Mayflower, twice, it was discovered that the Miller family has quite a bit of history written elsewhere.

Aunt Winifred thought a lot of her family and her nieces and nephews. She tried to save as much as she could for them, and bought bonds to be passed on to them when she died.

Her niece, Ruth, lived with her in Abingdon for a year, and then moved back with the boys to Arlington and bought a house on 30th Street. By 1957, both the Allen boys and our three children were in school full-time. But we were all living in areas that seemed to be on the edges of the school district.

Back to School

The early 1950s was a tough time for the children; each child attended a different school, being shifted around as necessary to keep the school districts evenly balanced. This was during a time of great influx of children ready to start school with not enough schools opening fast enough to accommodate all of them in the same school each year. Nevertheless, the children had good teachers and a solid education.

This roller coaster of new faces became the norm for me. Stratford Junior High School was for seventh- to ninth-grade students. The smarter seventh-graders would come into class already knowing their fundamentals, so this level of math became boring for them. One day I decided to challenge my sharper students by teaching them the role and importance of bases. In case people aren't aware, our math system consists of 10 symbols: 9 symbols (numbers 1-9) and zero. In base 12, we created two new symbols. Therefore, math became interesting and fun for the students because it forced them to think. One day, we would do our problems in base eight and another day in base seven and then in base 10.

The reason for practicing different bases was because eventually I got down to discussing base 2, which only consisted of 0 and 1. It was important that the students learn this, because these two symbols are the only reason we have binary systems today (computers) with two symbols; the electricity is either on or the electricity is off. Thus the number system was used in powers (2 to the power of 2 is 4, 2 to the power of 3 is 8, and so on). But this is enough of such now!

Eighth- and ninth-graders also learned algebra and geometry. I enjoyed making math a fun and challenging, yet vital, subject to know. It was a wonderful thing for seventh- and eighth-graders. But when they put modern math into elementary school, it was a disastrous situation: The students at this age were not learning the fundamentals they needed such as multiplication, addition, subtraction, division, and so forth. At this time, I had become chairman of the Math Department and felt that it was necessary to meet with the elementary school teachers to discuss the issue. We then made plans to remedy this situation. I asked the school administration for a remedial math teacher to help those children who needed to catch up.

Across the hall from me, the Spanish teacher, Marilyn Barrueta, had her classroom. For that year's Spring Break she was planning a trip to Spain for the children who were taking Advanced Spanish and invited me along to chaperone. The flight was uneventful as we landed in Madrid. I learned a few necessary Spanish words on the trip, such as "water" and "bathroom," which I have long since forgotten. It is true: if you don't use, you lose. I learned years later at a retired teachers' meeting that when she became quite ill at the end of the trip after drinking a bottled carbonated beverage, Mrs.

Barrueta gave credit to me for getting her and the students on the plane for our scheduled trip home.

While I was teaching math, I decided to try to increase my salary by studying for a master's degree in education, with special emphasis in home economics and math. At the time, I was making $15,000 a year. After school I would attend the University of Maryland School of Education. My sponsor was Ms. Spencer, a professor of education and home economics. Without her encouragement, I probably wouldn't have stuck to my studies, given the other responsibilities in my life. She realized my struggles with raising a family and working full time while pursuing a master's degree. My trek to Maryland became such a routine to the point where I could escape most of the red lights and get to class just in time.

Most of my time was now spent getting homework done and preparing lessons for my own students. It wasn't the most relaxing time of my life. I received my master's degree but did not take time to go to the graduation exercises (goal accomplished).

After I received my master's degree in 1958, I was asked to teach modern math and computers. Modern math was great for the smarter students where we studied the properties of the numbers; it was the equivalent of pre-algebra. I don't intend to let this book become a teaching lesson, so I'll leave it at that.

My teaching career lasted for 21 years at Stratford Junior High, until our children graduated from college. When I retired in 1974, my average salary for the last three years of teaching was $18,500, which was used to figure my pension benefits.

This is enough about my professional life at this time. I'd like to include some of the things that were going on in society.

Chapter Ten

Integrating Stratford

In 1954, two years after I started teaching at the newly built Stratford Junior High School, the Supreme Court of the United States made a momentous decision: All schools in the United States needed to be racially integrated. Unlike the southern states, this wasn't a problem for some northern schools that were already integrated. In some southern communities, including in Virginia, public schools closed rather than integrate.

Many states failed to respond to the *Brown v. Board of Education* decision in a timely manner. Virginia was one such state to resist this order, doing all it could to postpone the changes. Some of the parents that lived in Halls Hill, a black community in Arlington County, sued the school system for not integrating.

These were the same parents who were working for good schools in the '40s along with the Citizen's Committee for School Improvement (CCSI). The elected school board did improve the school system, yet nothing seemed to be equal between the still-segregated schools. It took the Circuit Court two years to act on this lawsuit.

A favorable ruling by the circuit court judge meant that Stratford Junior High School would be the school most involved, because the parents lived in that school district.

Since the superintendent of Arlington County schools and the principal of Stratford were both southern gentlemen, neither one wanted to integrate the school. The principal asked the teachers if we would be willing to teach black students. Some teachers refused. I personally felt it was an insult to be asked this kind of question, and I, of course, volunteered, considering it an honor to have these students in my classroom.

Finally, the judge ruled that four students from Halls Hill would be admitted to Stratford on February 2, 1959.

This caused an intense reaction in the community. Some realized the importance of the matter while others remained intensely opposed. Many meetings were held by people in the community, and a great deal of preparation was made by the school staff focusing on that date when four seventh-graders from Halls Hill would attend classes at our school.

The principal turned the issue over to the assistant principal because he wanted nothing to do with the matter. Assistant Principal Doris Matthews was an excellent disciplinarian: Students respected her and behaved well. She called the seventh-grade students together and talked with them about what was going to happen on February 2 when the black children would attend. She asked for student volunteers to escort the newcomers from class to class.

Three boys, Michael G. Jones, Ronald Deskins, and Lance D. Newman, and one girl, Gloria Thompson, arrived on February 2, 1959. The guidance counselor and the assistant principal each visited with the children and their parents in their homes to discuss what was expected to happen on that day.

Since the school had received threats, there were policemen on the grounds to escort teachers into the building from their parking spots. Each teacher had to have a pass in hand. This went on for weeks. With all this in mind, I think you can see how intense this situation was when I tell you that there were dozens of policemen in and around the building, and in the neighborhood in the time prior to the integration.

On the appointed day, the police escorted the new arrivals into the building through a remote entrance that was furthest away from the main entrance. Some of the parents were so afraid that something tragic was going to happen that they fearfully gathered at neighbors' homes. The student body accepted the change as part of a normal day: From the moment the black students walked in there was no indication of any conflict. There were some subtle differences: Teachers were to stand outside their classroom doors during class changes; any student going to the restroom needed to have a pass;

the black students were escorted to the restrooms since they didn't know where they were located; during lunchtime, the black students ate together at a separate table in the cafeteria.

Once the new students arrived, they were taken to the front office, split into pairs, and given their class schedules. Two were assigned to my first-period math class. The class accepted the newcomers without any fanfare. I welcomed them into class, showed them where they could sit, and we went into our lesson. It was just a regular day.

It only turned out that way because the entire staff had taken great pains to arrange that everything went smoothly. At other schools in the South, there were ugly confrontations.

After two years, these students were now ninth-graders and they wanted to plan their usual prom. The fear of some parents was that if they had it in the gym, the black students would be free to attend. Some of the parents organized a white prom and sold tickets for the event. One ticket was accidentally sold to a black student, and the issue was brought to the assistant principal. She called the boy in to her office to explain the matter to him, to retrieve the ticket, and to refund his money. Both were crying in the process, Doris Matthews later wrote.

History has recorded a lot of the tension in the communities. I won't attempt to detail that information, but I will say that the legislature, populated by those with mainly southern ideas, threw out the elected school board law that we had worked so tirelessly to pass. The governing body of Arlington County, whose members are elected, was then tasked with appointing members to the school board until 1992, when we again were permitted to elect our school board.

Approximately 25 years after the integration of the schools, the Legislature voted that a plaque be placed in Stratford Junior High School, indicating that it was the first school to be integrated in the Commonwealth of Virginia. When the plaque was hung in the library, the staff and students held a special program, and three of the original four black students returned for the celebration.

At this point, the former students were all involved in

professional activities in the field of their choice. Both students and parents were present; the only people missing were the teachers who taught the students during that time. Although no official invitation was issued, I was able to attend the event by chance. because of chance. I was to meet my friend Elizabeth Campbell at Stratford, which was near my home, to return the purse she had left in my car the night before. An organizer of the event gave 83-year-old Elizabeth a ride to the school and dropped her off in front of the building. Since I was waiting for her, I helped her from the car into the school building, and she invited me to stay with her for the meeting.

The program discussed the desegregation controversy and the disturbance it caused in the community. I felt it was necessary to give an account of the events on that day from inside the school; I stressed that it was a normal day like any other. Upon reflection, all of the children had handled the integration gracefully; it seemed that it had bothered the parents more.

Arlington County also recognized this anniversary by placing a sign in front of the school recognizing it as a historical spot for being the first integrated school in Virginia.

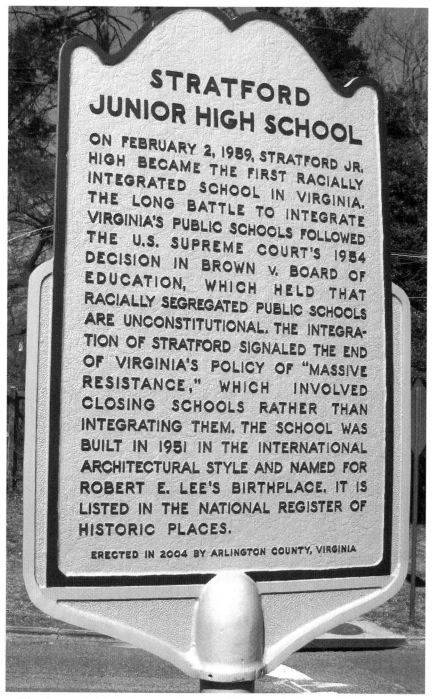

STRATFORD
JUNIOR HIGH SCHOOL

ON FEBRUARY 2, 1959, STRATFORD JR. HIGH BECAME THE FIRST RACIALLY INTEGRATED SCHOOL IN VIRGINIA. THE LONG BATTLE TO INTEGRATE VIRGINIA'S PUBLIC SCHOOLS FOLLOWED THE U.S. SUPREME COURT'S 1954 DECISION IN BROWN V. BOARD OF EDUCATION, WHICH HELD THAT RACIALLY SEGREGATED PUBLIC SCHOOLS ARE UNCONSTITUTIONAL. THE INTEGRA- TION OF STRATFORD SIGNALED THE END OF VIRGINIA'S POLICY OF "MASSIVE RESISTANCE," WHICH INVOLVED CLOSING SCHOOLS RATHER THAN INTEGRATING THEM. THE SCHOOL WAS BUILT IN 1951 IN THE INTERNATIONAL ARCHITECTURAL STYLE AND NAMED FOR ROBERT E. LEE'S BIRTHPLACE. IT IS LISTED IN THE NATIONAL REGISTER OF HISTORIC PLACES.

ERECTED IN 2004 BY ARLINGTON COUNTY, VIRGINIA

The county's historical marker outside Stratford, now H-B Woodlawn.

Chapter Eleven

The Joys of Parenthood

Home Movies

When the children started to arrive, we invested in a movie camera. As the children grew, we had a lot of fun taking pictures of their activities. We also purchased a movie projector and screen. The children loved to see themselves on the screen; they would laugh and giggle at themselves and each other while watching the movies.

Every year we gave each child his or her own birthday party; Margaret was the only one who had a summer birthday. On her first birthday, I had the party out in the yard and had made her an angel food cake. As I started to take a picture, she reached out and grabbed a fistful of cake. And so, her guests did the same thing. There was enough cake left around the candle, so we were able to light the candle and sing happy birthday. Since I had not iced (frosted) the cake, there was no problem of having messy hands. In later years this was the favorite movie they wanted to see because they had had so much fun.

The Neighbors

Our family enjoyed living in our small home on Quintana Street. The street came to an end, with just two houses standing between ours and the woods with a small stream at the bottom of the hill. The children enjoyed playing in the woods, where there were footpaths, a railroad track, pond and rock formations that invited all sorts of imaginative play. This seemed like a safe enough activity that I would let them go down to play on their own. We had just one rule: The children had to stay close enough to home in order to hear my whistle when I blew it, and then be home in the next five minutes.

Sometimes I would blow the whistle when they had been gone for quite a while. I wanted to be sure that they were all okay.

Every night before bed, we had story time with all five kids: Two on this side, two on that side and one in my lap. We took turns choosing what book to read. This perhaps helped the children to learn to read quicker than they might have otherwise.

A neighbor, living across the street and at the end, had two boys and they each had a red dump truck. The two boys were given the job of moving dirt from one spot to another so the family could have a level spot for parking their car. Malcolm and Margaret had lots of fun helping the boys with their job. The other three children were usually playing in the sandbox and at home and having a great time.

At the church, when the children were old enough, they started singing in the cherub choir. At this time the church was growing so fast that there were 40 children in the cherub choir, and when they sung in a group, they had their little choir robes to wear.

One interesting family whose children were also in the cherub choir was the Smiths. As mentioned before, we had a neighborhood full of children. This family needed to move to a larger house and the house next to us became vacant, so Irmingarde and Charles Smith bought the house next door. It seemed as though they were not having their own children, and they ended up adopting five kids, three boys and two girls. In addition to having a large family of her own, Irmingarde also drove 306 children back and forth to school each day covering 53 miles as a school bus driver for the county. What a busy life!! In the evenings, Irmingarde would visit us during our dinner time while Charles was supervising the children cleaning up after their meals. (He came home earlier than Drennan did, and so they ate earlier.) We had our own large and boisterous family that needed to eat. Eventually, when I made a comment about it not being convenient to receive visitors while we were having our dinner, she got the hint and stopped coming over while we were eating. Otherwise, we had a good relationship as neighbors. After several years, they felt the need of more space and found two acres with a house out in Fairfax. A new family with one girl moved in, and the daughter and Margaret became good friends.

Extracurricular Activities

As mentioned before, our children were taking lessons in ballet, tap dancing, and acrobatics. When they had developed enough skills, the teacher would put on recitals. In preparation for these recitals, I enjoyed sewing and putting together the costumes for our kids to wear. The recitals were held at the Ashton Heights Women's Club and were widely attended.

Our family did not take long leisurely vacations. How-

A dance recital.

ever, one year a client of Drennan's invited us to vacation at Chamberlain Hotel in Norfolk, Virginia. This was a real treat for the whole family! Here the children were able to lie flat on the piers while looking down in the water at the swimming fish, and they also tried to catch some of those fish as well. I also remember another vacation we took to Scientist Cliff (Maryland) on Chesapeake Bay. At the time we were visiting a family that had four boys – that was quite the experience! We all enjoyed visiting the cliff and thought it quite interesting to see the location of one of the world's richest fossil deposits.

Gardening

In the early '50s, I decided to order some earthworms and start a new project of organic gardening. One fall I ordered a load of what I hoped to be maple leaves (which were a more delicate food for the worms) from the county, and this pile was dumped in the driveway. In preparation for the arrival of the earthworms, I collected about eight fruit boxes and layered moistened leaves and added a handful of powdered limestone to make these boxes inviting for the worms to live and grow in. I set the fruit boxes on 2 x 4s in the corner of the garage next to the 20-cubic-foot freezer. Because I had stacked them on top of each other, the leaves would stay moist longer, and I would not have to water them as often.

Over time the earthworms would eat the leaves and produce castings through their digestive system, which they deposited in the box. I wanted to have them reproduce so that I could transfer them in large numbers to our new compost pile. Earthworms help to keep the soil aerated, and their castings make the soil rich for planting. The children helped create the compost pile by layering the remaining moistened leaves and handfuls of lime.

The earthworms laid eggs and reproduced quickly in this very rich environment, and I soon found that the boxes were full of earthworms. When this happened, we emptied them out along the edges of the compost pile that we had prepared in the corner of the yard. From there, the worms found their way into the compost and continued to grow. After time, we spread some of the compost pile with the castings over the garden, and worked it into the soil. This made the soil richer in nutrients and more productive.

Family Adventures

When I scratched my hand on a rusty nail before we took a long road trip, I thought I'd better get to a doctor. He gave me a shot for lockjaw, also known as tetanus. Aunt Winifred visited us from Illinois, and we made a trip with her to Rochester, New York, to see Ruth, who was still in the hospital. Imagine traveling with five preschoolers and their matronly great-aunt! At the time, there were no seatbelts in cars, so the children could move freely around the back seat.

On our way to Rochester, we passed through Moscow, Pennsylvania, and leaving to go north, we went up a long hill. At the foot of the hill, I saw that there was a gas station. When we got toward the top of the hill, I noticed that a red light had appeared on the dashboard, and I decided to make a U-turn and coast down the hill and stop at the gas station we had just passed. The man at the gas station took a look at the children in the backseat and at Winifred beside me and realized I was in a bad situation. He was about ready to close up shop, but when he saw my plight he said, "I'll see what I can do to help you." It turned out that I needed a new water hose, which he was able to install and sent us on our way. I never was so grateful as I was at that moment.

As I recall, Aunt Winifred stayed in Rochester for a short time, while we drove on to Evansville, Indiana. As we crossed Ohio, the red sweet cherries were ripe, and I bought some for us to eat. When we finally got to Evansville, I was breaking out in hives and went to a doctor for help. I told him about all of the cherries I had eaten on the way. As it turns out, I had a bad reaction to the tetanus shot, which was made from horse serum, and had to receive yet another injection to counteract my allergic reaction. This was quite an experience, as you can imagine!

We spent some time visiting Mother, where I recovered from the hives. Soon we were on our way without further incidents back to our home in Arlington.

Pets

While the children were growing up, we had some pets. For awhile, my husband wanted to have a bulldog. The bulldog was very nice and pleasant with the children, but when visitors came to the house, they were frightened and didn't want the dog to roam freely. Later on, the bulldog became pregnant, and because she was not able to deliver the

My mother, Minnie Stahl Riggs, age 82.

babies and we didn't have any spare money for an operation, we decided to have the veterinarian put the bulldog to sleep.

Later we bought a collie, which soon became the children's favorite pet. After some time, the collie had a fit and our vet prescribed medicine we gave her to end the seizures. Again, our experience with Lassie did not end well, but she was the children's favorite pet, and Malcolm particularly felt close to Lassie.

The children would often walk over to East Falls Church where there was a store called 5 cent 10 cent Store or to Westover to visit the Ayers Store to buy small items with their money. One day Malcolm asked if he could walk to Westover, and Lassie went with him. He left Lassie outside of Ayers, and when Malcolm left the store, he saw that Lassie was missing.

Malcolm was whistling and calling Lassie by name to

try to find her, and when that didn't work, he came home. After Malcolm told me what happened, we both went back to Westover to look for Lassie, and Malcolm cried the whole way there. While looking for the dog, I noticed a collie on one of the screened-in porches of one of houses prior to reaching Westover. When Malcolm whistled, the collie on the porch made no indication that she was our dog, so I did not feel free to knock on the door and ask about the collie. I told Malcolm that if they let the collie out, she would probably find her way home, but she never did show up. Deep down, I always felt that they stole the collie by getting it into their car. I'm sorry about the whole incident because she was in need of medicine that they did not have, and I've often wondered what happened to her.

Scouts

Scout Troop #104 has been a part of Clarendon United Methodist Church for many years, and is one of the oldest in Arlington County that is still in existence: It has the distinction of being continuously chartered for 94 years or more. We felt that the Boy Scouts of America was a worthwhile activity, and Malcolm and Drennan became involved in the organization.

After Malcolm had been in the Scouts for a while, they were having trouble getting leaders, so his father took some training to be qualified to help lead the boys. Mr. Mitchell, who also had a son in the same troop, and Drennan served together as Scoutmasters. Around this time, Cub Scouts were for boys in first grade and older, and once he reached 10 years old, Malcolm moved on to the Boy Scouts. One of the trips the Boy Scouts took was to Camp Roosevelt in the mountains. On this particular winter it was so cold that the shaving cream and potatoes froze, causing the troop to head back earlier than they planned.

Reilly Lewis, who is now our church organist, grew up near the church and belonged to this Scout troop as well. He was 11 when he went on this trip with the troop.

When Drennan came home with the frozen potatoes, I remember cooking them while they were still frozen, and they cooked up nicely. We had a lot of fried potatoes after that because I didn't want to waste anything. When Drennan's professional life became so busy that he stopped being a scoutmaster, he was given the usual "thank you," which was a scout standing on a pedestal.

Technology

Many young people were caught up with the newfangled invention: television. When TVs were coming on the market, there was a moment when I was really wishing that we had one: some big government event was being broadcast, and I wasn't able to see it. Since we never bought anything until we had the money for it, our purchase of a TV came later.

Once we had a television set, it became a distraction for our children. They were beginning to want to watch TV instead of study. Privately, Drennan said to me, "I'll take a tube out of the TV so it won't work."

This provided the time for the children to do their homework. The whole family did without TV for about a year. As the children progressed in school, they were doing well and saw the need, themselves, to spend time on their studies.

It was my privilege to stay home with the children for 15 years. This was a period where women were more likely to stay home until their children were all in school. In those days, mothers were not as focused on having a career and an income. Oftentimes, you can't send your children to college without some extra money. We had three in college at the same time.

Change

In the meantime, our children were approaching their teenage years, and we were feeling the need of a larger house for the family. The girls were together in one room, but one was neater than the other, so there was a bit of stress.

We soon found a house we liked, made an offer, and it was accepted.

Many years later, Drennan and I realized that our parenting had suited our children. Her friends started calling our older daughter Meg when she was in ninth grade, finding

Margaret too sophisticated. Once Meg was through college, married and in a home of her own, she wrote us the following letter. You cannot imagine our joy as we read it.

"Dear Mom & Dad,

I've wanted to let you both know about the appreciation and gratitude that I have been feeling toward you. Since we couldn't be together for Mother's Day; I didn't want to wait for Father's Day – and since the way you raised me was so intertwined with what you did together – I decided it would be most appropriate to write a joint letter and send it to you.

One of the things I have appreciated most about both of you has been your "where there is a will, there is a way!" philosophy of not giving up – but seeing that if you want a change (better schools) you have been willing to invest your time and energy to make good schools happen. I was really fortunate to have grown up in one of the best school systems of that time – and my life and competencies – and love for learning – have been greatly influenced by that. – Thank you!

This "get up and go" model you both have set has given me the belief and strength to see that I – one person – joining with others – can affect positive changes in my community to make things happen. This has given me a great deal of faith in myself as being worthwhile and faith in the system of change within our way of life. This way of handling life's problems, your respect for medicines, drugs and alcohol has encouraged me to depend on myself and not rely on some foreign substance to solve my problems. That alone, is a very important gift.

Another trait that I cherish and appreciate about you has been the way you both cared when friends and especially family have needed you. Your willingness to raise two additional children without asking what was in it for you. Your willingness to help each of us children when we have really needed the support. Winnie as her marriage fell apart, Mac in his drive to get credentials he wanted, and me in times when I've needed good old

R & R – rest and recreation.

Another source of strength has been the way you have encouraged each of us to develop our talents. I never cease to be amazed at the messages my female friends received around sex-role stereotyping. Neither of you ever told me I couldn't be anything I wanted to be. I have never felt one down in either talent, competency or ability because of being a woman. I'm finding that this is a rarity for my age group. Therefore – I've never felt I couldn't or shouldn't develop my talents – and that is really important to me.

I'll also never forget the numerous times, Dad with a bus fare – Mom in a store – when each of you displayed an honesty that is so rare. You each taught me that honesty is more important than money and that even if you're not charged it is your responsibility to make it right with the other person. I really treasure this part of each of you.

Along with this – but different too – is the trust you gave me during all my growing up – but particularly the teen years. Being trusted to make good decisions gave me a confidence in myself that is immeasurable. It felt so good to me then, and still feels good to me now.

Last, but not least is the way you both are curious and ask a lot of questions. Seeing you do this and allowing and encouraging me to do this has kept me from ever feeling ashamed of what I don't know – but instead taught me a love for figuring things out and learning new things from whatever sources are available.

I know I've been wordy – but I really want each of you to know that I love you and have a very deep appreciation for all the gifts you have given me – especially the gifts of character and "worthwhileness." These are gifts of parents who really care – and I want you to know that I know you do care. And to say Thank you! – thank you – from deep within my heart.

I love you,
Meg"

Chapter Twelve

Move to Huntington Street

We found a larger house in the more elite part of the county: the nice homes in the hills and valleys east of Westover Shopping Center. This area was about one mile closer to Washington, D.C., than where we were living, but still in the alphabetical, three-syllable street names section: "Quintana" was the "Q" while "Huntington" was one of the "H"s. Harrison Street, another "H," was heavily traveled.

One part of Huntington Street started at 17th Street at the crest of a hill, and was a block long to 18th Street. The houses on this part of Huntington Street all had an alley in the back. This was nice because you could drive into the garage from the alley and enter the house in the back. It was a special spot in the county since it was the second highest; the highest was the reservoir. I was happy that the house was not located where floodwaters could come up into it.

When we made the offer, I never dreamed that we would end up actually owning a home in Tara: the place where you always dreamed you could live but would never be able to afford. I always thought that we were buying a house in an area beyond our means. It was known as a nice place to own a house, kind of in the upper class. The other place that was considered the place to live was over by the golf course.

We made the offer several thousand dollars less than the asking price, figuring that we would never get the house anyway. It turned out that the people who owned the house were in the process of getting a divorce, so they were eager to take our offer and move out. After all the paperwork was finished, we wanted to do a few things in the house before actually moving in. The study walls were painted a deep red color, and we wanted those changed and a few other things one does before moving in.

We moved all the things we wanted to keep. Then, we took our time getting the house on Quintana Street ready to sell, which was about six months. We were able to move into the bigger house before selling the Quintana Street house because we had been saving for the down payment for a larger place. That way we didn't need to sell the smaller house in order to buy the other one.

We were able to pay the new mortgage two months in advance, which was a safety feature if I did not have the money to make a monthly payment. This turned out to our advantage: The mortgage was paid off earlier than it had to be, and we saved interest money in the process.

Also, by holding onto the Quintana Street house, we didn't have to take the first offer that came along. We were able to double our money. We originally rented the house with an option to buy, and in May 1941 the buying price was $6,500. We sold it in June 1958 for $14,500!

We made the offer to buy the larger house in the fall of 1957. Malcolm was in ninth grade and Margaret in eighth at Williamsburg Junior High, and Winifred was at Tuckahoe, one of the many elementary schools that the children were moved in and out of throughout their educational careers. Although we moved during the middle of the school year, the children were able to finish at the schools they were attending. The next fall, Malcolm moved to Washington-Lee High School, and the girls attended Swanson Junior High.

We moved in on New Year's Eve of that year. Frances and Dusty Rhodes, close friends from Purdue who lived a few miles away, dropped in to see the house just as we'd moved in. They had a house of their own that was on an acre of land and had a tennis court. Whenever Francie would call—and it was daily—Drennan would say, "Your girlfriend's on the phone." He never said it in a disgusting way, but always gave me time to have my conversations with her.

That evening I made the comment that it looked as though the fireplace in the living room had never been used, so Drennan took a rolled up newspaper, lit the corner of it, and held it to the bricks in the back, making some smoke on them. To me it indicated that we were going to use the fireplaces. We had a total of three: in the living room, the study, and the rec room in the basement.

Frances and Dusty didn't stay long that evening, but brought something along to eat so we could celebrate our move into the house. It was a surprise, and a very fun thing for them to have done.

Our new home was made of brick with a curved walkway leading up to the front door. When you came inside, you entered a hallway. This led straight to the dinette (breakfast nook) area with a door that could be closed. On the left side of the hallway was a large 24-foot living room with a big picture window on the front of the house. The fireplace was at the end of the living room. The dining room was next to the living room, with a door leading to a screened-in porch that extended into the back yard. On the right hand side of the hallway was a closet and a door that opened into the study. There were also stairs up to the second level.

Our Huntington Street house.

Across the back of the house were the dining room, kitchen, dinette, and hallway to the garage: If we had been shopping, we could bring groceries right into the kitchen from the garage. There was also a stairway to a room above the study; this was meant to be the maid's quarters. From the dinette, there was a hallway that led into a bathroom with a shower stall. In the front of this part of the house was the study with a picture window and a fireplace.

On the second floor, over the main part of the house, there were four rooms: three nice-sized bedrooms and one small room with a closet and a window. There was also a pink bathroom with a linen closet. We each got settled in our rooms. Ours had the stairway to the third floor.

The third floor was a full stand-up space that was large enough for two bedrooms and a bathroom to be added if we ever needed it. However, we used it partly as a library. Drennan, with his ability to do woodwork, built bookcases that he put on wheels; they rolled back and forth in a track system so that you could access the books on the back shelves.

The reason that we needed this storage space was because Drennan had a special interest in collecting books for reference. One collection was all of the Supreme Court reports from the beginning; the first few years were leather-bound. The other set was the Interstate Commerce Commission reports. He was a specialist in interstate commerce law, which covered all of the rules that pertained to transportation rates (rail, truck, etc.) for getting merchandise all over the United States. (I gave them all to George Mason University Law School after he died. I was given a $10,000 tax deduction that year, since I had them appraised.)

He was also one of the lawyers who worked to establish a communications system for our federal government. At one time, a senator introduced a bill to have the telephone systems be more useful to the government. When this bill was passed, it was sent to Government Services Administration, where Drennan was employed, to be put into effect. Part of his work was to help create a system that was usable by the government for conducting business over the telephone.

This was eventually done with a coded telephone system, so that people in the government could have privacy when communicating. This meant that government workers did not have to travel to different places to do business. It saved a tremendous amount of time and money for our government. I understood it to be millions of dollars. I thought this bit of history was interesting.

In order to get to the basement, which was the fourth large area of the house, we took the stairs down from the breakfast nook. The basement, which was under the entire house, consisted of a fireplace room, the recreation room, the laundry room, and the carpentry/furnace room. An interesting note is that since the house was being built for a gas-light company official, the house was not only equipped with a gas furnace and water heater but all the appliances used gas. There was an exit door from the recreation room to the backyard, which was accessed by an exterior stairwell. Typical of the time, the basement had a window and a window well at each end to let in light.

There was a half bath and a closet underneath the inside stairs with shelves for storing photo equipment and other items seldom used. The laundry room was large enough to hold a 20-cubic-foot freezer. In the carpentry room, there was enough space for Drennan to have all of his special saws and equipment. In the recreation room, we had a ping-pong table. Along one wall was a built-in bench with a lid that lifted up for storing things underneath. This was to sit on most of the time. The two main rooms were finished with pine paneling and the floors were also nicely finished. We all enjoyed this part of the house. In fact, the family enjoyed living in this solidly built house — our home for 31 wonderful years.

After we moved in, my attention turned to doing some interior decorating. While I solicited the help of an interior decorator, Drennan was focused on building cabinets on either side of the large window in the study. He was also planning to install a sound system with the equipment controls in the study so we could hear music in different parts of the house.

When I needed to make decisions on buying furniture, he would go with me and help make the final decision. We bought a small upright piano and put it in the living room across from the bay window. The children started taking piano lessons from a music teacher named Martha Hedges, who lived one block down the hill and whose husband built their house with a large music room for recitals. The Hedges had a daughter the same age as Meg, which helped lead to a lifelong friendship between the two families. To this day, Malcolm still enjoys playing the piano. Since the school had a music program that involved children learning to play instruments, each child chose an instrument to learn to play. Malcolm chose the trombone, Meg the viola, and Winifred the flute. At one point Meg didn't want to carry her viola back and forth to school and she talked me into buying her a second viola.

I got ahead of myself in the last paragraph talking about the children's musical development, but now, back to decorating and furnishing the Huntington Street house. An interior decorator helped me pick out material for the draperies in the living room, with matching wallpaper for the dining room walls. We bought a mirror to hang over the fireplace with blue trim to match the draperies. Two beautiful cabinets were used to hold the speakers for music in the living room. These were placed on either side of the fireplace. We bought a beautiful rug and a dining room set called Georgetown Gallery Mahogany Suite.

By flipping a switch in the study we could have music in several different rooms. When Drennan finished making the cabinets for the study, he bought two pieces of slate to fit on top of the lower cabinets. The fireplace in this room was fitted with glass doors, which could be closed at night when we wanted to go to bed.

Now that you've had the inside tour, I'll share some interesting details about the house that we had moved into: first, it was built by a builder for his brother, who was an employee of the Washington Gas Light Company. Every time we turned around to do something to the house, we marveled at how well it had been built. The plumb line lined up perfectly with the vertical lines formed by the windows and door frames. It was the best built house I'd ever known. This helped confirm that we'd made a good buy.

Secondly, the brother and his wife had some input on the building process. Every time I went to wash those large windows, I rejoiced and said to myself, "I'm sure glad she won out on getting one large piece of glass as the windows, instead of individual panes." However, when we were on the screened-in porch that did not have a door that let us go into the backyard, I always thought: "Why did he have to win out on this point?"

Actually, I felt that the inside of the house was more interesting to look at than the outside. An ivy vine growing on the side of the front door hid a bare spot that looked as though it needed a window. It was soon pointed out to us that it was not a good idea to keep the ivy on the house because the roots would loosen the mortar in between the bricks. So we ended up removing the ivy plant completely.

Eventually, the evergreen tree that was growing out front helped to camouflage the bare area. There was also a gas-powered air-conditioning unit in the front of the house that was cleverly hidden by shrubbery.

The house was on a corner lot and was beautifully landscaped with shrubbery all the way around it, and with a hedge along the alley. There were also five pin oak trees in the front and side yards. After several years of living there, we discovered that pin oak trees needed to be sprayed for a fungus so that they wouldn't die. We had them sprayed for several years. We soon realized that this was too big a job to do any good. Gradually, as they began to die, we had the larger branches removed and had lots of wood for the fireplaces. The trunks of the trees were so large across that we sold them to people who could cut them up and sell the firewood; they took the stump away, too, so that we could have a smooth lawn area. We planted a maple tree in the front yard.

Soon after we moved into the house, we planted an apple tree in the backyard between the porch and the hedge. This was planted to provide shade to the back porch. Over the years, the apple tree grew, and we kept trimming the top branches back so they did not hang over the hedge and drop apples in the alley. It turned out that this tree had a short trunk and was easy for the children to climb in addition to presenting a beautiful white bouquet when in bloom. It also produced lots of apples for applesauce and eating. At the same time we planted a cherry tree on the other side of the garage; it did not produce much fruit for us as the birds liked cherries too.

Our apple tree.

A number of years later, I felt the need to have azalea bushes along the side of the house to match the ones that were in front; there were all a beautiful pink-red color. About this time, I went to see a friend in the hospital, Ruth Cox. I mentioned the fact that I'd like to have more azaleas of the same color along the side of the house. She immediately said, "I can tell you how to do it!" I went home and followed her directions. I prepared a tray about 1 foot by 2 feet with reasonably rich soil and then I clipped 36 twigs off of the azalea plants in front. I put the twigs into the soil with the proper amount of moisture. I took some green bamboo and made some mini-arches as supports. This formed a frame over the twigs so that I could put plastic over the top to keep the moisture in but also let the light go through.

I put the tray on the screened-in porch so that it would have some sun in the morning, but shade in the afternoon. We went on a trip and I remember coming back home and thinking, "Oh, everything is probably dead and I've wasted my efforts." When I went to the porch and pulled back the plastic, I saw that all of the twigs had rooted! I transplanted them to small pots, and when they were large enough by the springtime, I planted some on the side of the house. I had enough to give away, too.

I don't want to bore you with too many details, but the rest of the house was gradually furnished. As time passed, there were other items that were added.

For example, when Aunt Winifred died, Drennan drove to Illinois. He helped close the house in which she had lived all her life. Since the family lived some distance away, they decided to sell the house furnished. Members of the family took what they wanted and were able to move. Drennan loaded the car with all he could. He particularly wanted the drop-leaf mahogany table that was a family heirloom. He was able to get it into the car along with a lot of other family treasures that I will mention later.

We only lived a few blocks from Arlington Hospital. The numerical address for the hospital and our home were the same, so we were constantly getting the hospital's mail! The family really enjoyed living here on Huntington Street, and we shared our home with many friends and groups over the years. To justify having this lovely home, I always felt that sharing it with friends and other groups for large and small meetings meant that we were being good stewards of our resources.

Chapter Thirteen

Shifting Gears

W hat does it mean to shift gears in life? I am referring to the different stages of family life. First we are
married, then we have children, and we shift gears.
When they go to school, we shift gears. When they go off to
college, the family becomes just two again. All through life,
we're changing how we're living. Although my husband preferred to stay at home and read, he really was involved in
things outside the home besides working for better schools. A
summary he wrote of his life said:

"Born 1909 in Illiniois. Resident of Arlington, Va. since
1937...Graduate Grinnell College, B.A. 1931; Post-Graduate
Illinois Univ. College of Law, 1932-4; Graduate Georgetown
Law School, L.L.B., 1935. Qualified as National Red Cross
life saving examiner in 1929, and as water safety instructor
in 1955. Was varsity team swimmer in college, and worked
as life guard at a municipal pool. Other Activities: President,
Arlington Camera Club 1942-3; President, Arlington Better
Government League 1947-8; active in Arlington Citizens
Committee for School Improvement as legislation chairman
from 1946; chairman of several committees in Arlington
Civic Federation, and was awarded Star Cup Trophy by
Federation in 1950; was Asst. SM and Scoutmaster Arlington
troop 104, 1954-7. Member of Arlington Committee of 100,
was Chairman 1969-70, and served on its board of directors.
Member of Virginia State Bar, Federal Bar Assn., and
National Lawyers Club. Listed in "Who's Who in South and
Southeast, 1973-1974." Stratford Harbour: Property owner
since 1969; Chairman of Steering Committee to organize
Property Owners Association, 1971; First President of
Association, 1972; and a member of Board of Directors as
Immediate Past President from 1973."

I would like to interject here the success that my husband was having in his career. In the mid-1950s, he accepted a new position in the federal government and worked his way up to what today is called the Senior Executive Service. In July 1962, he received a Meritorious Service Award from the General Services Administration. He was cited for his "unusual ability in the overall planning and administration of the development and implementation of transportation management, communications and public utilities programs" for the agency and for testimony to Congress that resulted in GSA losing less appropriation than a congressional committee had recommended. In addition, he made invaluable recommendations that led to more efficient operations, reduced backlogs and put in place other highly qualified key personnel.

The award concluded with the following:

> "While serving as Special Assistant to the Commissioner, and in his most recent appointment as Deputy Commissioner, Transportation and Communications Service, he has, without exception, performed in an exemplary manner in fully sharing in the over-all planning and administration of the development and implementation of all transportation management, communications and public utilities programs of the General Services Administration.
>
> Mr. Miller's knowledge of the programs of this Service, his devotion to duty shown by his numerous hours of overtime, loyalty and experience gained in previous positions make him an irreplaceable official of this Service."

Imagine that: Irreplaceable. That was my husband. I was so proud of him, my jaw literally dropped when I read about his award at the ceremony.

Because I had finished my master's degree and was prepared to teach the modern math that was being considered for schools, I was asked to teach it. Part of the course of study for seventh-graders was the beginning of computers. I was teaching seventh-graders how to write little programs for the computer so that we could set up loops and do the simple things that you can do on computers. At that time, when computers were beginning to come into use, one of my little seventh- graders said to me, "Mrs. Miller, I could write computer programs that could take money right out of the bank."

I stood back and looked at him and said, "But you wouldn't do it, would you?"

He was very smart, went into high-school-level math in junior high, and college-level math in high school. This is the rest of the story: He went to Stanford University to do his graduate work, and sometime later someone in California was writing and doing things that really messed up other people's computers. As it was being broadcast in the news, and his name was reported, I first thought that it was my seventh-grade student. I finally realized that the last names were slightly different. My student's name ended in "son," and I was very relieved that my former student was not involved in this situation.

As the students wrote their little programs for the computer, we would telephone them into a big room where the computer run by the county school system would test them to see if they would run. Now in this short 40-plus year span of time we have gone to computers that you can hold in your hands. Before that, one computer took up a whole room!

About the same time that Drennan received his award, we had planned a 25th wedding anniversary celebration as a family event in our new home. I don't remember all of the details, but our son Malcolm dressed up in formal clothes at the age of 19 and was the host for the party. Meg and Winifred dressed up for the occasion, too, and were helping to serve the food to the guests.

The table looked beautiful with a flower arrangement, as well as the good silverware, etc. There was also a lot of good food to eat. This was a special occasion and lots of fun.

During their high school days, both Malcolm and Meg were doing some dating. Malcolm had a Unitarian girlfriend, who he later said made him think about his life more. Meg

Meg, me, Drennan and Malcolm at our 25ᵗʰ wedding anniversary celebration.

was seeing someone, and she knew that she had a curfew of midnight. Years later, she said to me that she was grateful for it. You don't normally hear that from your child, but she was glad that they had a curfew! Both Meg and Malcolm were very active in the yearbook and involved in many school activities. Winifred, on the other hand, preferred to stay at home with a good book, just as her father did.

Malcolm graduated from Washington-Lee in 1961, Meg in '62, and Winifred in '64. We never spent much time or money deciding where they would go to college, never really talked about it; in the end they each decided that they would go to Purdue. Meg remembers becoming interested in Purdue after seeing some Purdue memorabilia in the attic, especially my Gold Pepper paddle. She ended up becoming a Gold Pepper herself while at Purdue.

Even though Malcolm and Meg were at the same university, Purdue was a big school and they didn't see much of each other on campus the first year, but the next two years they saw more of each other.

When Winifred talked about going to college two years later, she considered Purdue and Michigan State University. She decided to apply to Michigan State University in East

Lansing and was accepted.

In the spring of Malcolm's junior year, he said he didn't want to be an electrical engineer, but after our advising and insisting that he get his degree, he finished his fourth year at Purdue and graduated. Then he went into the Peace Corps to give himself some time to decide what he really wanted to do and be in life.

The summer that Malcolm graduated from Purdue, both he and Meg were out of school and at home. During her junior year at Purdue, Meg had become engaged to Phil Filiatrault, and he was planning to go into the Air Force when he graduated from Purdue.

One day, the following incident happened: From the dining room of our Huntington Street house, the door was left open onto the screened porch, and since it was summer, it never occurred to us that this was a problem. This particular morning, Meg had arranged to take a flight; I got up and took her to the airport at 5 a.m. Someone must have noticed us drive off and that there was no other car around, but there was an open door. He cut the screen, slashing down and across the bottom of it, crawled onto the porch, and walked in. He did not know that Drennan and Malcolm were still there asleep, so he ventured upstairs. Drennan heard a noise and he said, "Malcolm, is that you?" He realized that the person had turned and run and that meant someone else was in the house. He jumped out of bed, followed him, and as the thief ran out towards the back door, he bumped his arm and dropped my sterling silverware set on the floor. By the time I got back from the airport, the police were taking fingerprints from the silverware box and other places that the thief might have touched. He evidently came upstairs to find a pocketbook to steal some money. They didn't have much evidence to find out who it was. But later, the police reported that there had been a series of robberies through the area of more expensive homes. They did eventually catch the person, and we were told that he was looking for money to support his drug habit.

Malcolm spent the summer preparing for service in the Peace Corps, and he left that fall for Malaysia. He was assigned to a school that was comparable to one of our high schools. Some of the students that he taught math and carpentry to were native boys who traveled to the nearest facility for their learning. In a way, Malcolm was also a student as he continued to learn the native language.

During his two years there, Malcolm kept in communication with us by sending home pictures, letters, and recorded voice tapes telling us what he was doing. He mentioned how he went home with some of the students to visit them on weekends; he was always exploring and interested in finding out what they needed to learn. I might interject here that when Malcolm was done with his Peace Corps tour, he decided to do some sightseeing on his way home. He made it to 26 different countries with just a backpack. (He had sent his things home in a trunk.) He brought home some wonderful presents: Thai silk from which I made a dress; two blue vases from Italy, which were very heavy! I never understood how he was able to do all of this.

The Peace Corps came into existence after John F. Kennedy was elected president and challenged college students to give something of themselves by living and working in other countries to further peace and understanding among nations. I remember very vividly JFK being elected president. (At this time, Drennan's work was of the nature that we were invited to an Inaugural Ball.) Kennedy was very promising as the youngest person ever to be elected to that office. In his Inaugural speech, he made the following statement, which I thought was a wonderful thing for people to ponder:

"A strong America cannot neglect the aspirations of its citizens—the welfare of the needy, the health care of the elderly, the education of the young. For we are not developing the nation's wealth for its own sake. Wealth is the means—and people are the ends."

I remember distinctly where I was when I heard the news of his being assassinated: I was standing in the hallway outside my classroom and was deeply saddened to hear that this had happened.

Barbara Jones penned a very touching poem, "Special Delivery from Heaven," a fictional message from JFK to his family after he died. You can go online and read it; I would have put it in this book, but it has a copyright!

During Meg's senior year at Purdue, we were making plans for her wedding. She and Phil set their date for June 26, 1966, which was just a few weeks after their graduation from Purdue. We reserved the Clarendon United Methodist Church for the occasion. We had almost a year to plan the details, and it was during this time that I made her dress and veil, and fashioned a full-length train from three yards of French lace.

Meg in her wedding gown with her parents and sister Winifred.

They had a beautiful wedding and reception at the church. Phil's family came in from Milwaukee, Wisconsin, for the occasion. Meg had three bridesmaids, with her sister, Winifred as her maid of honor. I made her dress, too. Phil had three brothers and they were all a part of the wedding party.

Right around this time, Winifred was a sophomore at Michigan State University in East Lansing, Michigan, and was enjoying her time in college. She met Bob Payne, a student just one year ahead of her, and after some time they planned to get married. They finally decided on the date of August 5, 1967; she would complete her junior year by this time. Bob was training as a Navy officer as well as finishing his senior year, and he wanted to be married before he left for duty sometime after his graduation in 1967.

This gave me time to make her wedding dress and veil. She wore the same lace train that her sister had worn the year before. Bob had three sisters who were all in the wedding as her bridesmaids. Each of them made their own dresses from the same pattern. Meg was Winifred's matron of honor. I made her dress, too.

They also had a beautiful wedding at Clarendon United Methodist Church and a nice reception after the ceremony. Drennan was the proud father and photographer

Bob was soon stationed in Meridian, Mississippi, and Winifred joined him for the summer; that fall she went back to Michigan to complete her education. After she graduated in 1968, Bob returned from his duty station, and they settled in Michigan.

The '60s were known as the turbulent decade. Young people were rebelling and making their own decisions, which did not make it easier for parents to be effective. Fortunately, our children did not tend to follow their peer group very closely. Early on, Malcolm, our son, had begun to rebel by smoking. Drennan and I talked about this, and we told him that if he were going to do this then he needed to smoke at home as well. Our philosophy was that we wanted to see what his habits were. He never did smoke at home but told us later that he had continued his habit through college and the Peace Corps. It turned out that he had a bad case of bronchitis, and it became necessary for him to stop smoking for it to clear up. He discovered that he felt better, and he decided to quit smoking altogether. For this, I was very grateful.

Now that the children were educated and out on their

own, it was time for us to shift gears again and think about our own future activities.

Drennan "Retires"

Drennan finished his work at the General Services Administration in 1968. As many of you know, people who get high up in government are often "retired" because the new administration coming in wants to hire its own people. Drennan had served through many other party changes without being disturbed by the upheaval. But this time, the powers that be asked him to leave. Since they retired him early, he was given additional compensation in the form of a special bonus, which has paid off financially all these years.

Soon after retiring, he made the remark that this would probably save his life for some time to come because he had tremendous stress and responsibilities in his job.

Drennan started doing all of the cooking for our meals. I said to him, "It's wonderful that you are doing the cooking; could you please do the shopping, too? I think it's best that you buy the groceries for what you want to cook." This was good for him to have something special to do every day. It was wonderful for me to come home and not have to worry about cooking. I was always having gourmet meals to eat and enjoyed sitting down at the table not knowing what to expect! Women who knew of my situation were jealous of me because they were still having to do their own cooking. But, I cleaned up the kitchen afterwards, did the laundry, trimmed the shrubberies, sewed, and painted where necessary. We had a wonderful division of labors.

Since I wanted to reach a certain number of years teaching so that I could have better retirement benefits, my plan was to keep working. When the chairman of the Math Department retired, it seemed that I was next in line to step into that position at Stratford Junior High. I taught algebra and geometry, the highest math at the junior-high level. I also taught math during summer school. All these things contributed to my retirement benefits. In addition, I had a ninth-grade homeroom class. I was being recognized for my abilities, and I was enjoying my work and my students.

During this time, we ventured into the surrounding areas of Virginia looking for land to invest in, so that we could have a place away from the city. In many areas of the state there were new developments by American Central Association that included recreation centers where there would be good places to have a summer home.

We bought some land near the beginning of Skyline Drive that was up on a hill not far from the Shenandoah River. We went canoeing on one of our recreational jaunts, which we'd never done before. We also explored the recreational opportunities in the other direction near the Potomac River. Stratford Harbour was there and sounded quite interesting. It was located between the river and the home of the Lee family about 95 miles away from the Arlington area. Stratford Harbour had many different facilities: a boat marina, a stocked lake for fishing, river beaches, tennis courts, swimming pool, and a clubhouse. They had even built a dam to form the lake, and the road that went around the lake was on top of the dam. You could build on the lakeshore or the river shore. There was also a golf course not too far away. Once we were land owners, Drennan became very instrumental in transferring the property from American Central into the hands of the property owners' association. His work on its behalf saved the association close to a million dollars. This was because of his knowledge of state and federal laws related to land ownership.

Montross was the closest village to Stratford Harbour. It had a post office, a bank, a grocery store, a few nice places to eat out—all the little necessities for living. Local people in that area liked to come and enjoy the facilities at Stratford Harbour too, so they bought land and helped increase the development's popularity. Wherever there's water, the land near it becomes more valuable, and we believed that Stratford Harbour was a good investment. We gradually shifted from the original lots that we bought to other lots that became available: one particular lot was on a point that went out into the lake so that we could see all the way to the headwaters of the lake in one direction and to the dam in the other. We had another plot across the lake that included five acres on the hills and valleys. This particular piece of land had only one building site because of the drainage and septic issues. I encouraged Drennan to choose a plot and a building plan. I never wanted to force my preference, which would have been the lake-view plot. I think Drennan would have preferred the other plot. In the end, health issues kept us from building: Drennan knew that he wouldn't be close to a doctor that far from the city. I was able to get a good price for the properties many years later.

The land we had purchased near the Shenandoah River never developed in the way Stratford Harbour did. My businesswoman's instinct was that someone would be interested in it eventually. Years later, I was able to hold out for the best price when it was the only lot that they needed to buy to complete their land ownership for future development.

Naturally, as I got closer to the end of my teaching days, my desire to retire was increasing, and Drennan was encouraging me in that direction so that we could travel and enjoy life together. I finally retired two years before usual retirement age. When both of us had the freedom of time to do the things we wanted to do, we found the retirement years very enjoyable and exciting.

Chapter Fourteen

Looking Ahead

By this time, the grandchildren had started arriving. David, the first, was born in Omaha, Nebraska, in November 1969. His parents, Meg and Phil, said, "We have a beautiful red-headed boy!" We were able to fly out to be with them, but only for a weekend because I was still teaching.

Winifred and Bob welcomed Brian in June 1971 in Michigan. When Brian was about a year old, it became clear that Winifred and Bob's relationship was not going well. They divorced shortly thereafter, and Winifred and Brian came to live with us on Huntington Street. During this time, Bob made two trips from Michigan to bring Winifred's things to our house; the items all fit into the basement fireplace room nicely.

Grandson David Filiatrault with his grandparents.

Meg and Phil moved to Landisville, Pennsylvania, about a 2½-hour drive from us, in 1970. She taught school another year before the arrival of their second son, Mike, who was born in September 1972. They also had a daughter, Annette, in April 1975. We got together more often as the children got older. We were fortunate to be able to see all of our grandchildren growing up since they were nearby. It was a joy to be grandparents without the responsibilities of parenting.

I decided to retire at the end of the school year in 1974. When I retired, I was a ninth-grade homeroom teacher and taught five classes of math. I was mainly a ninth-grade teacher, so I participated in most of the ninth-grade activities, including helping to plan the prom. At the end of the year, they honored me by planting a tree in my name. This was a wonderful thing for them to have done! I'm sure they got this idea because I always had plants in the classroom. My room was located on the south side of the building where the sun came in brightly. I would start my tomato plants in my classroom early in the spring, and the students would help me water them.

It was a tradition for the ninth-grade class to publish the yearbook called the Cavalier. I enjoyed taking many pictures for their book and helping them with this project.

At the graduation exercise, the Cavalier staff also gave me "The Most Dedicated Teacher" award. The retiring teachers were given a Certificate of Appreciation signed by the School Board Chairman and the Superintendent of Schools. The Arlington Retired Teachers Association gave a lovely tea for all the retiring teachers, which introduced us to this very active organization.

During my teaching years at Stratford Junior High School.

As I was retiring, the legislature was working on making amendments to the Retirement Act. This was very helpful in improving the benefits for retired teachers. At the same time, the county started a local benefit for teachers as well. One thing that was very helpful for me is that I got paid for all of the sick days that I had not used. This totaled $7,000, and I got to buy into my local retirement plan with this money. I was retiring late in the 20th century, and the Commonwealth legislature was just getting around to making sure that teachers had better benefits.

This is how my husband summarized my retirement in our Christmas letter:

"Martha Ann retired at the end of the school year last June, after more than 20 years of teaching at Stratford Junior High School in Arlington; but not abruptly, because she is easing out of teaching by doing some substituting in the nearby high schools. She is kept busy as a member of the Church Board and in other church activities; a delegate to the county Civic Federation from A.A.U.W.; member of Delta Kappa Gamma, the teachers' honorary sorority; and in catching up with 20 years of some housekeeping."

No one had wanted to take the presidency of the local chapter of Delta Kappa Gamma, so I just stepped in and got them organized.

That first summer our interests seemed to turn to sailing. We decided to go to the Annapolis Sailing School to take lessons. After some experience sailing, we learned to sail on the Chesapeake Bay and spent a week there on a sailboat. One special learning experience was what to do when the big ocean liners came up the bay heading for Baltimore. When there is no wind, don't try to do anything, but let the liners steer around. We experienced a storm coming up and were taught how to anchor so that none of the student boats would run into each other. At one point, they said we might be sitting here for a day. What in the world would we do with ourselves? But the time passed and we fed ourselves, relaxed, and slept. It was an enjoyable outing.

This whole time I wore a life jacket because I didn't know how to swim. I could float a bit, but I wasn't anxious to be in the water. Another thing that helped me to enjoy these outings was the fact that my husband was a skilled swimmer. He had been on the varsity swim team, and he was also trained as a lifeguard. If Drennan had been as I was, rather unskilled in the water, I certainly would not have been as comfortable out there on the water.

Later on in June of 1976, we decided to go to the British Virgin Islands to participate in a special week-long sailing course where the Annapolis school had private property. We flew to the islands and soon met the others who would be a part of our class. We would have instruction during the day, but at night the teacher would go back to the head boat and we would sleep in our boat by ourselves. It was fun to sail from island to island. Each one had its own little store with items we could buy, such as crackers and peanut butter. I cannot say that we had a good diet on this trip.

One day during our time with the instructor, I was steering the 34-foot motorized sloop, and I noticed there was something running along the floor of the cabin. I brought it to the instructor's attention, and he said, "Turn off the motor!" It was motor oil leaking out. He called back to headquarters and said that we would be coming in, and that he wanted someone there to meet us who would repair the boat. Fortunately, the wind was going our way, and we were able to get back to the base with only our sails. In short order, the people fixed the motor and sent us on our way.

The whole trip was an unforgettable experience. The water was clear, it was beautiful sailing weather, and the dolphins were jumping up out of the water ahead of the sailboat, which made it all a wonderful time of sailing. This area was one of the prime yachting places of the world, with good weather, steady winds, fine beaches, and anchoring places with restaurants. I noted when we landed and took off that the landing strips for the planes were very narrow and short, so I was very grateful when the plane was in the air taking us back to the States.

During August, we spent two weeks in Hawaii visiting the islands of Oahu, Kauai, and Maui, as well as the big island of Hawaii. One thing I'll never forget is the road to Hana on Maui. It was a narrow, winding road that you would drive up in the morning and back in the afternoon. There were many beautiful waterfalls along the way. I was glad that I was driving because I probably felt safer knowing that I was in charge of getting us around those curves rather than trying to sit quietly in the passenger seat.

After this tour, we flew to California where we spent 10 days, including a week of visiting with Malcolm. While working for his Ph.D., he had been required to study another language. He was able to use the Malaysian language as one of his requirements since he had learned it while he was in the Peace Corps. After Malcolm got his Ph.D. in psychology at George Washington University, he moved to California, where he had to take exams in California and intern with a practicing psychologist before he could get his license to practice there. He finished up his requirements and established his own practice. He still lives in California today.

Before he had moved from Arlington, he wrote the following citation, which he had framed. It has hung on the wall in our home ever since. Here is what he wrote:

The University of Life
has conferred upon
MALCOLM DRENNAN MILLER
MARTHA ANN MILLER
the Degree of
DOCTORATE OF PARENTAL SUCCESS
For their contribution to strengthening the educational
system, their encouragement, and their support in the
educational and growth endeavors of their son
Given this fourth day of May in the year
of our Lord nineteen hundred seventy-five

Malcolm R. Miller
(Your loving son)

He lived in Santa Rosa, and at that time, he had a couple of acres up on a ridge and two dogs. We stayed part of the time in a cottage on the Russian River in a redwood grove. We made a thorough tour of Sonoma County's wineries.

Since we were on the West Coast, we decided to travel a little further north to Idaho to visit Drennan's sister, Esther, and her professor husband, Ivan Nye. They took us to Glacier National Park (Montana), where we saw the sights and engaged in Ivan's favorite sport of fishing. He had always promised me that he would take me fishing one day. We caught a dozen rainbow trout that first day, each weighing about a pound.

When we went out the next day, the idea was to try to catch something a little bigger and to have fun pulling it in. Since Ivan was an excellent fisherman, he had knowledge of where to go to catch all varieties of fish. He took us to a completely different lake to find Dolly Varden trout. We paddled the canoe several miles, or so it seemed, to the headwaters of the lake. This is where the fresh water running down from the mountainsides enters the lake. Once we were in place, Ivan baited the hook and cast the line. He got a strike: a six-pound fish. I said, "That's what I want to do." So, he baited the hook for me, cast the line, and handed it to me. A strike! I really wanted to do the casting myself, and told him so. Again, he put on the bait, and then I cast the line. Another strike! This time I reeled in a 7 ½-pounder!

This was the biggest fish I'd ever caught in my life, and it was a real thrill to have a chance to do it. If you know anything about fishing, the reeling in of the fish is the fun part. I haven't done enough fishing to know all of the techniques or their names, but my early experiences tantalized me to be able to find even bigger places to fish than our small pond.

I got the strike immediately because the fish jumped for the hook right away. I played with him ever so gently, but persistently, to get him closer to the canoe. As soon as he was close enough to the boat, someone grabbed a net and put it in the water and under the fish to bring him inside the boat. It's always such a thrill to go fishing and have a special catch.

After others had a chance to fish and no one else was getting a strike, we decided to head home, which meant paddling back to where the car was parked. On the way home, we had a special treat in that Ivan knew a restaurant that would prepare our fish for our dinner. We gave them one of the three fish and they cleaned it and fried it for our dinner along with some slaw and French fries. This gave us a good chance to visit as we waited for the fish to be cooked. This was one of the most memorable fishing trips I have ever gone on.

While we had been away, Winifred was taking care of the house. She had earned her accounting degree, and in January 1977, began employment with the National Automobile Dealers Association in McLean, Virginia, first in analyses of reports of dealers. She then moved up to become a junior accountant with the association. She and Bruce Kriebel got married on March 26. Interesting note: my two daughters and I had now gotten

Rewards of our fishing trip with Ivan Nye, right.

married on the 26th day of the month of our birthdays. Bruce was a native of Pennsylvania, a graduate of American University in accounting and was employed with the CIA in computer programming for its administrative offices. They moved to Alexandria for a short time with Brian, who was in first grade. Later, they bought a house in the Arlington area.

Brian spent his early days growing up in Clarendon United Methodist Church. He was known as the "little, curly-red-haired boy." There became a time when there were not many teenagers his age at Clarendon, so the family switched over to Westover Baptist Church, where there were more teenagers. When Brian went to college, he went to Michigan State, since his father, Bob, was a resident. Brian now lives in Michigan and works at a television station.

We bought the shell of a new Ford van in March of 1977 with the idea that Drennan would make it into a travel vehicle. It had double doors in the back and on the right side, as well as the passenger and driver doors up front. Across the back of the van, Drennan built a framework that held a full-sized mattress. We used the space underneath the frame for storing our supplies and clothing. We could access these areas from inside the van.

On the right side there was a little sink with a drain that went down to a pail below that we could empty outside the van through the double doors. We used the sink to wash up or do dishes. On the left side of the van was a little refrigerator that I think was somehow connected to the engine, which kept it running and cold. Maybe it was a battery, I'm not sure. My husband took care of those details. But, I certainly enjoyed having it. We also had a commode.

The best part about the whole van was that we ordered two captain's seats that swiveled around for us to sit on. When we traveled we were very comfortable. We even had the equipment to listen to beautiful music. On the ceiling behind the captain's seats, Drennan put up a track so that I could hang some draperies. We were also able to have privacy when we stopped for the night because he attached curtains that I had made to the windows.

In May and June we motored to Illinois for the 50-year high school reunions of two high schools that Drennan attended. We enjoyed these occasions more than anticipated and met many old friends; I met some new ones. Also, we visited my family and friends in Wisconsin. We spent Drennan's birthday in the town where he was born and camped in the yard of Edith Graves, who was his next door neighbor and a young lady when he was born. She was close to 90 at the time of this trip, and Drennan had a very special relationship with her that he cherished. As a result of our visit, we now have a cut-glass dish from Edith. These are now collector's items. The rest of the time was spent sightseeing, visiting all of the towns (except one) where Drennan had lived before leaving for college, and doing genealogical research.

That fall, I made a trip to Evansville, Indiana—my hometown—visiting friends along the way, but primarily to do genealogical research of my family. I visited many relatives and accumulated considerable information about my four sets of great-grandparents who came to America about 1840 from Ireland, England, Germany, and Switzerland. I also had a nice reunion luncheon with elementary school classmates.

Son-in-law Philip Filiatrault had finished his graduate studies at Pennsylvania State University Capital Campus; we attended the commencement where he received his Master's degree in Business Administration. Eventually, Meg also completed her qualifications for being a school psychologist.

On one occasion, we went to Pennsylvania to take care of the children while Meg and Phil took a few days of winter vacation to Florida. The purpose of the trip was for the parents of the local Scout troop to get together for an outing. They traveled by bus. Meg had arranged for a woman to come in and be with our grandchildren on Sunday afternoon until she and Phil arrived home that evening. That way we could get back to Arlington by Sunday evening. While we were staying there, there was a big snowstorm. We left at our planned time and drove back to Arlington on a road that had been snowplowed and only one lane was open in each direction. We had called ahead to have one of our neighbor boys shovel our walk so we could get into the house.

After we got home, Meg called us from Richmond and said the bus had broken down. They arranged with Bruce,

Winifred's husband, to drive to Richmond and bring them to Arlington. I was to drive them from Arlington to Landisville that night. I laid down on the davenport to get a few hours of sleep until they arrived. As soon as they got in, they woke me up and we left right away. Since this was a night with snow on the ground, there were only few landmarks. I followed a truck that was ahead of me a block or two because I could see his red tail lights. We arrived in Landisville early in the morning. When I got them home, they went to grab a couple hours of sleep. Since the pipes in the kitchen were frozen, I got a hairdryer and held the warm air on the pipes until the water started running through. I was able to catch a few hours of sleep and then drove back to Arlington that morning. This was quite an adventure.

A few years after I retired, Drennan was still doing the cooking and I continued doing my jobs at home. One day he said to me, "I think it's time that you take over the cooking again." "Honey," I replied, "I cooked for you for 35 years; you've got a long way to go yet." Fortunately for me, he continued doing the cooking, but he bought umpteen number of cookbooks, so another collection was begun in our house! But, I felt that if that was what he needed to keep cooking, then so be it.

He kept his exercise by walking to Westover shopping center to pick up a few things, and then had a fairly steep hill to get back to our house. Remember? It was up on the second highest point in the county. Then he would walk in the other direction along Harrison Street to the Lee-Harrison shopping center on Lee Highway to get any other groceries that he needed.

When the grandchildren would come to visit, they always asked him to make their favorite dish: cashew chicken. It left him with a lot of responsibility when they came to visit, but he would make it for them. I would make the desserts and other specialty things such as apple pie. Another thing that they particularly loved to do was to climb the apple tree in the backyard. It was ideal for climbing because it had a short trunk and then the big limbs went out from that, about 3 feet off the ground. Those limbs were strong enough that they could climb from there up high. When those June apples were ripe, we would make applesauce. When Mike was about 10 years old, he gave us a wonderful image of his memories of those times.

FROZEN APPLESAUCE

At Grandma's   house, there
was a giant apple tree in the back yard. The branches
were low enough for us kids to get up and climb into the
tree. It was one of my favorite things to do when I was there.
On that tree sour green apples grew. We would pick and collect
the apples and the whole family joined into making applesauce.
We would peel and core the apples. Grandma, Mom, and Aunt
Winnie would supervise cooking down the apples. As each
batch of apples finished cooking, they were poured into a
conical sieve with a special roller. That's where Dave,
Annette, Brian, and I would stir and mash the cooked
apples through the sieves with the rollers. The mash
that was collected on the other side was packaged in
plastic boxes and frozen. We made enough
applesauce to last all year long. It was best
served frozen because we could eat it
like ice cream. Sweet, melt in
your mouth,   goodness.

- Mike Filiatrault

Interspersed through the '70s and '80s while the extended family activities were going on, the two of us took a number of special trips. Drennan would also plan those since I had gotten more active in community activities.

Chapter Fifteen

Adventures of Travel

Africa

The first big trip we took was to Africa in October 1975. It was a sightseeing tour and photography safari in and around Kenya and Tanzania. We had signed up with a tour group and flew into Nairobi, the capital of Kenya. The next day, the Kenyan president was speaking outdoors to a large group that was sitting on bleachers on the side of a hill. All of a sudden someone yelled, "Bees!" Immediately, the crowd panicked, leaving the bleachers and running in all directions because they seemed to think that if they got stung by one of these bees, it would probably mean death. We were standing near an elevated flower bed full of native plants, figuring that the people could not knock it down since it was secured with wires, and they would have to run around it and us. We found out later that one member of our party, a woman, did get knocked down and had to go to the hospital. We were fortunate to not have been on the bleachers.

We traveled from Nairobi to Tsavo National Park, then to Mombassa, where we saw the coral reefs in the Indian Ocean, a first-time experience for us. My memory fails me on how we viewed it, but I believe we had glass-bottomed boats so we were able to see the unusual development of the coral. They all seemed to be light-colored. They were beautiful, and it was the best coral reef that we saw on any of our travels.

In preparation for the trip, Drennan had equipped me with two cameras: one for close-ups and one for distance. We both took pictures, but because I had the better eyesight, I used two cameras. This trip was planned for the dry season because that was when the animals came in to the watering holes. When we started the photography safari part of our tour, we were in a Land Rover with one other couple, the Warfells. A friendship developed that continued over many years. The Land Rover was made so that the roof of the vehicle could be rolled back and we could stand up to take our pictures. It was like being in a motorized cage for us to be safe in while we watched the animals running free. Our driver knew where to find the animals, and leopards often roam solitarily. All of a sudden he said, "Oh, I think I see a leopard," and he drove us across the area to a large tree. Up in the branches was a sleeping leopard with its legs dangling over the limb.

We stayed in cabins. At some places, the owner of the cabins would press a buzzer that went off in our rooms to call us whenever the animals were starting to come in to the water hole, sometimes in the middle of the night. The elephants usually came in to the water hole with their babies at night. But, since it was night, we couldn't take any pictures. For that visit, we were awakened at one o'clock in the morning.

I kept wondering where the water came from that was in the water holes during the dry weather. Why didn't it dry up? I guess that God provided for them as they needed. I was always grateful to know that the water holes were there for them.

It's interesting to note that all through the trip we noticed that the mothers and babies stayed together in groups, while the males were off on their own. The animal babies have to stay with their mothers to learn everything that they need to know.

The excitement of being in Africa was seeing all of the animals! We traveled to

Lions in Africa.

196

Ngorongoro Crater, which is one of the world's largest, measuring 10 to 12 miles across and being 2,000 feet deep. The height of the rim is about 7,600 feet, and it is surrounded by volcanic highlands with six peaks that rise to more than 10,000 feet. We rode in a Land Rover to different areas in the crater. Nature had created the crater hundreds of thousands of years before. Whatever animals were in the crater usually stayed there. Ngorongoro is known for its wildlife: zebra, gazelle, wildebeest—at the time numbering between 10,000 and 14,000 according to the time of the year—lion, leopard, jackal, rhinoceros, elephant, buffalo, and hippopotamus.

We stayed at a fancy hotel that served us dinner with silver furnishings. This seemed very unusual for the middle of Africa where you are there to see the animals. I was surprised that we sat down at the table with so many utensils!

We finished our tour in Africa at the Mount Kenya Safari Club, founded by actor William Holden. I was tremendously impressed by this beauty spot in the middle of Africa, not very far from the Equator. Peacocks, guinea hens, and other species of animals were wandering around in the yard. Mr. Holden wasn't there at the time, so the property was open to tourists. We stayed a few nights there. It was just a beautiful space for him to go to relax.

As we left Africa, we were excited to have flown over the pyramids, which we could see from the airplane. This trip was such an interesting experience that if I ever returned to a place I have visited before, this would be it.

Eastern Europe

During August 1977 we traveled with a tour group by bus through Eastern Europe. From that year's Christmas letter:

"We went through Yugoslavia, Bulgaria, Hungary, Romania, Czechoslovakia, and Austria, staying about three days in each of the capitals of those countries and also visiting other cities and towns. All of these countries have beautiful cities and lovely palaces and old-time resorts. Villages were interesting, with do-it-yourself architecture and construction: rough masonry covered with stucco and red tile roofs. Private ownership of housing is encouraged, and in rural areas, private ownership of small plots of land is permitted. Young people migrate to the cities, and in large cities there are immense developments of new condominium apartments and in some countries there is private ownership of apartment units. The communist countries have little unemployment. Wages are low, but prices of basic foods, housing and transportation are kept low, education and health care are mostly free, but prices for manufactured goods and imports are high. Restorations of historical and good old buildings are at a high level of activity, including churches which also are of great historical and artistic value. There is freedom of religion, but also education against religion. We sensed repressions of the communist governments, lack of competition, and the effects of anti-American propaganda for the past 30 years or so. On the other hand, our tour guides constantly reminded us of the resistance of these peoples against the oppressions and cruelties of foreign invaders for hundreds of years, and this desire for freedom inevitably will prevail. For them communism was a step toward freedom by freeing them from the remnants of feudalism."

Before we got to Budapest, the tour leader said that we could ask for different services there, such as pedicure or manicure. We stayed on the Pest side of Budapest, which is on the Danube River. At the end of the bridge crossing over from the Buda side to the other side of the river there is a hotel, where we stayed. They were assigning rooms to all of the different people on the tour, but they never called our name. They finally took us to the side and said, "We don't want you to talk about your room. Most of the people have very small rooms, and we don't want them to be irate."

We had a suite of rooms that was usually reserved for visiting diplomats! There were seven balconies that bordered the corner of the hotel. We could see from any direction that we wanted. There were also several entrances to the suite. The bed was very large and had draperies hanging next to it from the ceiling so you could pull them around the bed at night.

On the Buda side are the big government buildings. As we traveled from country to country by bus, I was impressed with the number of churches and their steeples. It was interesting to see so many churches in communist countries. Driving through our country, you don't see that many steeples.

Since this was in August, we traveled during my birthday. At one of our stops while we were eating, the entire restaurant sang "Happy Birthday" to me! I never knew quite who revealed that it was my birthday, but they did acknowledge it. This made it a special time for me for my birthday to be recognized.

We had special entrance into each country and special exit. There was a routine to entering and leaving the country. The only one that was particularly exciting was our experience leaving Czechoslovakia. On our way out of Czechoslovakia, the tour leader said to us: "Do not make any noises to try and hurry the process of us getting through, no noises or whistling, or they will delay us even longer."

There was a man with a gun and a dog near the gate that we needed to get through. They took one of the ladies off of the bus and told her that they knew about all of her cut-glass purchases. She had asked others to bring them out of the country for her so that she wouldn't have to pay the tariff. It turned out that they charged her more to take it out of the country than it had cost to purchase!

We went from there to Austria, where we visited the many beautiful sights in Vienna before ending our journey in Zagreb, Croatia, then part of Yugoslavia.

China

In 1980, China was opened up to any foreigners wanting to visit the country. Meg called me one Sunday and said, "Mom, we can't afford to go to China, but we thought maybe you could. Dr. Taylor made an announcement in church today that he's getting a trip together, and if you want to go, we'll sign you up." Dr. Norman Taylor was a professor at Franklin and Marshall College who taught Chinese culture and economics. He also spoke one of the dominant languages. Drennan and I talked about it for five minutes and called her right back. We didn't want the slots to fill up so that we missed this special opportunity to go to China with someone who spoke a Chinese language.

This was more than just a tour for sightseeing. Dr. Taylor was a specialist in China and Japan. This was in conjunction with the International Institute of Learning, where he would take students who would then earn credit hours for being on the trip. We flew from Washington, D.C., to Lancaster, Pennsylvania, where we met and took a limousine to New York to fly to Los Angeles, and then to Hong Kong.

There were 17 of us who made the trip. It was a nice-sized group to travel with. Before we left home, Drennan took along two particular pictures: one of the two of us, and one of himself. We flew into Hong Kong, a very international city. When we were there, it was known as the "Pearl of the Orient." Drennan stopped to talk to an artist on the street and asked him, "Do you paint from photographs?"

I assume that the man spoke English because they were able to communicate. The artist replied that he could paint the pictures, and said, "I'll have them painted when you return, and if you don't like them when you see them, you don't have to take them."

When we came back from China, we met with him and decided to purchase the paintings because they looked wonderful. We framed them upon our return to the States, and they have hung on our walls ever since. We spent three days in Hong Kong sightseeing. While in Hong Kong we went to Victoria Peak, the highest point where we could look over the harbor into Canton. This was a real experience in itself.

From Hong Kong we traveled three hours by train to get into China. Most of our travel through China was either by train or plane. The distances were so great that we mainly flew. We spent the day in Canton visiting a museum and temple. From there we flew to China's capital of Beijing.

In the morning, we went to visit Tiananmen Square and the Imperial Palace. Both are located in the middle of Peking, now called Beijing. Tiananmen Square, which can hold a million people, was named when the People's Republic of China was established. It is one of the largest squares of any city in the world. There is a monument built of white marble in the center of it. Each side is carved with information about different events in Chinese history.

As we approached the Imperial Palace from the square, there were many white marble steps leading up to the main gate, through which we needed to enter. Since this was an international study group, we were allowed to see more of the Imperial Palace than many regular tour groups. The palace covers 178 acres by itself. If one were to tour the entire area, it would take four days to see it all. The Imperial Palace was called The Forbidden City by the people because they could not enter it. During the Ming Dynasty, the Emperor claimed to be the son of God and to have super powers. Some of the names in the palace reflect this relationship: The Hall of Supreme Harmony, the Palace of Heavenly Purity, the Palace of Earthly Tranquility.

While visiting Peking we stayed in the dormitory of a school just outside the city. The students had to double up and make their rooms available to us. We were served wonderful meals for the several days we were there, while the students had to walk across the courtyard to get their bowls of rice. It was hard to justify eating the meals we were served when we realized that this was not the common diet. The last evening we were there they served us Peking duck, which was special to us.

It was a joy to walk on the Great Wall. There were parts of the wall that were being repaired, but it is considered one of the Seven Wonders of the World, so we wouldn't have missed it. It is a winding roadway through mountainous areas, with small buildings along the way that were once used by military guards. Horses used to haul ammunition and other things along the wall, which is five horses wide. It has a rich history.

It seems that long ago many small kingdoms began to erect walls to keep themselves safe. Once the emperor united all of the lands, he decreed that the people had to connect all of the little portions of the wall into one structure. It was begun in B.C. 200s and finished in A.D. 1300s. It stretches for over 3,000 miles, the longest wall in the world.

We also saw the Ming Tombs where 13 emperors are buried. Each tomb had its own entrance. There is intricate marble work, roof tiling, and many statues.

In Shanghai, I distinctly remember that the Chinese people would go out on the street and do their exercise. More and more of them kept joining the others to do their physical fitness. Shanghai is the largest city in China, and the most westernized. It was often referred to as the New York City of China. "Shanghai" as the name indicates is "high" and located above sea level even though it is a port city.

The Great Wall.

We only saw one other group of American tourists on the train going from one place to another. They were from Washington state, and we traveled for about half an hour on the train with them. This just indicates how special this trip was that China had not been open to many foreigners.

When we returned, our friends from Arlington were very anxious to hear about our trip since the country had been closed to outsiders for all those years. I recorded a voice tape to go along with a slide show that I put together. We bought what we needed to allow me to just press a button to advance the slides while the tape played. As a side note, technology tried to interfere with my making of the tape: when I attempted to record myself on the cassette tape and played it back, I kept hearing voices other than my own. It turned out that because we lived very near a television tower, I was picking up some transmissions. When I called the station and told them my problem, they made some adjustments and I was able to continue.

I presented the China program 21 times. While writing this book, I came across thank you notes from many churches, retirement homes, and civic groups where I had given the program.

One could write much more about China and the places where we visited. But I feel I must move on to other countries of travel.

Japan

In 1986, Dr. Taylor was invited to visit Japan to help celebrate the 100-year anniversary of a school started in 1886 by two students who had graduated from Franklin and Marshall College. They entered a seminary school, and when they became pastors they went to northern Japan to start a boys' school. Dr. Taylor planned another study tour, and we joined him on this trip to Japan. Japan is a very remarkable country, and the Japanese are a fantastic people.

From supplemental material about Japan provided by Dr. Taylor:

"The people are basically contented and happy. Crime is far lower than in most urbanized countries. Though the land is intensely crowded, everything operates briskly and without confusion. Society is stable and moves along smoothly. The democratic political system, while operating in many ways quite differently from our own, produces the necessary decisions and efficiently provides the services it should. All in all, it would be hard to find any large country in our contemporary world that runs more efficiently, smoothly, fairly and openly than Japan."

After the celebration at the school, we traveled south. It was interesting to see the different areas and observe the activities of the people. It was there that I was introduced to the popular food of Japan: sushi (raw fish). There is a first time for everything. I did enjoy it. There are a variety of fish products that were served in their cuisine.

My impression of Japan was a beautiful island with God's gift of nature, which melded the sea with the mountains. For example, Mount Fuji rises from the ocean to more than 12,000 feet above sea level; it is a magnificent thing to see! As a country the Japanese have tried to meld old-fashioned traditions with the technologies of a modern, developing world. A statement was made that Japan was the second most literate country in the world because they focused on educating their youth and people. The biggest city in Japan is Tokyo, one of the largest metropolitan areas in the world. It contained one-tenth of the population of Japan when we were there. All of the corporations and banks had their main offices in Tokyo, and it was known to have more than 100 colleges and universities in its boundaries.

The physical manmade beauty of Japan is breathtaking as well. The Great Buddha stands 53 feet tall and weighs 450 tons; many gardens dot the island, and as a gardener I marveled at how the white rocks in the landscaping did not have a single speck of dirt on them. The other aspects of the gardens—statues, shrubs, paths—displayed a pattern of beauty. It was interesting to see how they put things together to please the eye.

Russia and More

In 1987, another special trip developed after we received a call one Saturday morning. The person on the other end of the line said that she was going to take people on a trip to the Soviet Union and began telling me a little about herself.

Since her mother had grown up on the Red Square, and her mother and husband were going with her, it would make it special. Since it was a turbulent time to go to Russia, we never would have thought about going there without someone who knew her way around. Plus, we had already put down a non-refundable deposit on a trip to England. We considered all this and called her back and said, "Yes, we would like to go."

How she got our phone number, or even knew that we might be interested, I'll never know. It turned out that Elizabeth Baylor Neatrour was more knowledgeable about Russia than I had dreamed; she was very accomplished and had received awards on bettering relationships between the U.S. and the U.S.S.R.

It was a privilege to go with her. The trip lasted from May 19 until June 4, 1987. It included stops in Lithuania, Poland, East and West Berlin, and Finland. We spent about 2½ days in each city, enjoying the sights.

When we were staying at the hotel on the Red Square, we

Typical Russian onion domes.

had to leave our keys in our room. I thought, "What are keys for?!" I had a beautiful red hand-painted scarf that was stolen from my suitcase. (I should never have taken it with me.) We were cautioned to never venture out into the Red Square without the tour group. I never questioned this instruction.

The beautiful buildings and their architecture were interesting. I was impressed with the gold domes.

Since I was asked by several people before we left to bring them back some of the famous Russian nesting boxes, I was continually reminding our tour leader that I wanted to find a place to buy them. I also wanted to get one for each of my children and myself. We went to a small village near Moscow where they specialize in the art of making lacquer designs on papier-mache items, including the desired boxes. These are very elaborate drawings, and it takes quite a while for them to be made. So, it was no surprise that they were very expensive. I was able to get one for each of the children, but ended up just buying a book for myself on how they were made. It was in Russian, but was full of wonderful pictures, and I still have it today.

As we traveled by train from Moscow to Leningrad, I was wondering what they were trying to hide because the window blind was down in our sleeping berth. I peeked out from behind it, and all I saw was landscape and occasionally an old rickety house with a few trees and some livestock around the house. I felt sorry for the people who lived there because I could see it was a very poor area.

While traveling we had to be careful that we never touched our mouth with anything that had water, even when we showered. We had to use the sterilized (boiled) water that they put in pitchers in our room to brush our teeth because we didn't dare take it from the faucets; the water was infested with bacteria.

In Leningrad, there was a beautiful museum that we could have spent days and days in and never seen all of the treasures it contained.

We traveled to Vilnius, the capital of Lithuania (which means "Amberland") and then went by sleeper train to Warsaw,

Poland.

Warsaw, another capital city, was rebuilt on the ashes and rubble of World War II.

Berlin was very interesting. We had to get visas to cross from West Berlin into East Berlin. While we were in West Berlin, they allowed us to look over the top of the Berlin Wall. We could see the second wall that ran alongside the first one, making an extra barrier for anyone who would try to escape. It certainly gave us good insight into how the people were living in the communist countries.

We also visited a museum that contained all of the cruel ways in which people were punished for anything they might have done wrong, according to the law. It was unbelievable what man was doing to other human beings. It made me cringe to think that anyone would do such things to another person.

It is interesting to note that 2½ years after we saw the Berlin Wall it was demolished, and the two sides of Berlin came back together. The people in Germany were glad to see that wall come down!

I never talked to my German friend, whom I met while her husband was an ambassador in Washington, D.C., about how she felt about the wall coming down. Helga Hirsch and I became friends through an American Association of University Women (AAUW) outreach whereby our unit helped the embassy women navigate society in this country: where to find a doctor; how to make a telephone call; figuring out how to ride the Metro. We got the names of the different embassy women through a group in Washington. Not all of the women accepted the invitation, but many of them did, and we formed three groups so that we were never too many for meeting in each other's homes. Bridge seemed to be a new game for the German women, and when a couple of them said they wanted to learn how to play I volunteered to teach them since I love to teach.

During the time that Helga and her husband, Hans, were in the country, several of their children came over to the United States to go to college. Once Helga and Hans returned to

Germany, they would make trips back to the U.S. to visit with their children. They always arranged to get together with me whenever they were in town.

When I let her know that we had arranged to make a trip to see the 1990 production of the famous passion play in Oberammergau, Germany—it's performed every 10 years— she said that she would meet us and we could spend some time together riding down the Rhine River.

Chapter Sixteen

What Next?

T he '80s were a busy decade because I became much more involved with the American Association of University Women. In the early '80s, the AAUW headquarters sent out notices that it had a prize of one week for two people at one of five spas for the individuals who got the most new members that year. To me that was a challenge, and I thought, "Oh, this would be fun to do." So, I had a supply of membership applications and another flier in my bag that told a little about AAUW. Everywhere I went, particularly to the grocery store, I would approach smart-looking women who probably had graduated from college and who might have a child in a grocery cart. I tried to develop a conversation and gain as much knowledge about the individual as I could, particularly her telephone number. I figured she didn't have a lot of time to talk at the grocery store, so if I had her number, I could call her at a more convenient time. I was not focused on shopping for groceries during these outings.

I was having a fun time, and as the numbers grew, I thought, "Maybe I could win a trip to a spa." This would be a new experience for both Drennan and me. So, I was successful in getting 42 new members for our branch. As it turned out, two women had gotten a few more members than I had. The top person got to choose her spa location first, and I was hoping no one would choose Lake Geneva in Wisconsin.

As luck would have it, I got to choose this spa at Lake Geneva. I wanted that one because it was only a few miles away from where my brother, Arthur, was serving as a pastor. When I checked with my brother, they were going to be away when we needed to get to the spa, but he said we could stay in their house overnight, and then go to the spa early the first morning.

My brother, the Rev. William Arthur Riggs.

We enjoyed three meals a day for the next five days. We had chosen the "regular diet" plan, as opposed to a reducing diet plan. There were also all the benefits of being at a spa. We participated in all the activities. This was a special and relaxing time for both of us, and a new experience as well.

At the end of the week, when Arthur and Nancy had returned from a Methodist conference, we spent the weekend visiting with them—what an enjoyable time!

About that time, I was elected Treasurer of our local AAUW branch, and then elected a year later to the State Board, also as the Treasurer. I served in both of these positions at the same time, but I liked my math, so it was all right.

I then served as President of our local unit from 1986-1988. During this time of being in these offices, I was attending the state, regional, and national conventions. At one of the conventions in California, they voted to establish the Advocacy Fund. This was to help women who had been in their jobs and were eligible for tenure, but were not receiving it in the same way as the men in that company. So, this gave women a source of money to sue, if necessary, their employers. Everyone who was there and wrote out a check for $100 was considered a founding member of the Advocacy Fund. It helped many women to be treated fairly in their jobs.

AAUW has been working for "equity for women" for 130 years, and it looks like we will still be working for equity for some time to come. After attending my first AAUW convention in Boston, Massachusetts, I had observed a woman making a report to the conference who was over 90 years of age. I commented at the time: "That is what I want to do when I am in my 90s." It is interesting to note as I write this that I attended a convention in Washington, D.C., when I was almost 100 years old and was recognized as being the oldest member present. We went to a soundproof room for them to interview me before putting it on the AAUW website recognizing me as a longtime active member. It was in June 2011, and was still on the website as of the writing of this book.

In 1987 the local branch started a Research and Projects grant in my honor. This is a source of funding for people in the community to apply for money to do a particular project of interest. For example, if a teacher wants to work with a group of students to research something, she or he can apply and receive some money to assist. According to AAUW procedures, the branch had five years to raise $37,500 for the grant to become active. To my surprise, they accomplished this in three years, which I thought was a reflection of their appreciation of the many hours I'd been spending in AAUW activities. The grant is still active and, as I am writing this, is over $52,000. I learned later that my friend, Doris Moore, had suggested that the grant be started in my name.

After finishing being President, another opportunity for leadership came up. The Macy's Department Store was opening new stores in the Washington area. Each time they planned to open a new store, they would have a "Benefit Day" before the official opening of the store. The idea was to acquaint the community with the new store and give organizations an opportunity to earn money with this special project. The grand prize was a $5,000 cash award to the organization that got the most people in the store that day. The plan was for organizations in the community to sell tickets to people so that they could get in the store the day before the official opening.

I took on this challenge and chaired this AAUW project. There were 12 branches located in Northern Virginia, and I led the collaboration of these branches. The first year we participated, we didn't get the grand prize, but each branch got to keep the $5 ticket price for each Benefit Day ticket it sold. We all felt that this was a very neat project and a way to earn money for our 501(c)(3) scholarship fund, so we continued on. Because we were a well-organized group of women who worked together, we began to win the grand prize. I did not keep count of the number of Macy's stores that were opened, but for several years in a row we won it. In the end, we raised $87,000 for scholarship money for women.

In 1999, I met my granddaughter-in-law-to-be, Katrina Osterholdt, at her wedding shower. When we discovered that we both had an AAUW connection, we were especially drawn to each other. I have appreciated my time with this organization.

It might be interesting to note here that all of my civic activities in the community ended up being honored by the Arlington County Commission on the Status of Women in 1997. The Commission screens nominees and gives its Person of Vision award to people in Arlington who have contributed to the betterment of women.

I never dreamed of even being considered for, let alone awarded, this honor. In 1997, the superintendent of schools also was honored by the Commission because he had done so much for women teachers. Mary Margaret Whipple, who had served on the school board, the county board and became a Virginia state senator, as well as Elizabeth Campbell, who had started the local public broadcasting station, WETA, were among the caliber of honorees over the years. This is why it was so surprising to me that I had received it because they had done such big things. It seemed that I became more well-known after I received this Person of Vision award.

I continued to go to the Arlington Retired Teachers' Association meetings and learned that they were creating scholarships for students who wanted to go into teaching as a profession. It was important to me to support those who wanted to become teachers. This organization has meant more to me as time has gone on because they closely monitor what the legislature is doing and how it affects teachers' retirements and salaries.

My husband was busy working on his genealogy with a Kaypro computer, which was growing in popularity. It had its problems, but there was a club of people who owned the Kaypro computers, and they would get together to share their experiences about how to fix some of the many bugs.

As we approached our 80s, we received information regarding home healthcare. Through ARTA, we were introduced to a state-recommended agent who was selling home healthcare insurance. Since there seemed to be no guidelines on this new concept of buying home healthcare insurance, some of the companies were selling it and said that the premiums would never go up. But one would have to be careful because if expenses went up, and the premiums didn't, it meant that the business could run out of money. Our contract did not say that; we had a better policy. As I will explain later, this was a very important step that we took while we were still in the age-range to be eligible to buy this coverage.

Sandwiched in among these other activities, we used our van to make a 13,000-mile trip west. We took a route across the middle states (Indiana, Illinois) driving through Utah and continuing to the West Coast. Here we were, driving through Utah, no other cars on the road, with the classical music playing on our stereo, driving across land which was white like snow because of the salt deposits. We saw Grand Canyon from the north and south sides.

As we got to California, we also went far enough south to

see Bryce Canyon in the southern part, which I thought was more beautiful than Grand Canyon. Then we traveled up the route closest to the Pacific Ocean to Washington state, stopping at camping locations along the way.

We traveled to Vancouver and saw the Butchart Gardens, which are marvelous collections of flowers and plants from all over the world. For example, there is a Japanese Garden and an Italian Garden with specimens from those parts of the world. The significance of Butchart Gardens is that a woman put many hours into developing a beauty spot where her husband was responsible for mining lime. She searched the world to bring plants and flowers of every kind to her gardens. There were all sorts of plants that I had never heard of. We took a lot of pictures; everything was so beautiful. Fountains and hanging baskets were right where they should have been. There was a grandchild keeping up the tradition when we visited.

From there we drove to see Jasper National Park in British Columbia. Along the way we saw unusual animals and some were running; since this was open territory they could roam this part of Canada freely.

We headed toward South Dakota, where we saw the Badlands and Mount Rushmore. Some people may not know what the Badlands are; I didn't. At first I was not very much impressed with the Badlands, but once I understood what had happened there, I became more impressed. People had tried to populate this area, but because there was no water available, life could not exist. As my assistant and I read more about the Badlands in trying to write this book, I came across a story about two men whose lives were saved when their traveling companions covered them with sand to help them maintain the moisture in their bodies until the rescue party could come back with some water to give to them.

It was a beautiful sight to see the faces of the presidents carved in stone at Mount Rushmore. We were fortunate enough to be at a place in South Dakota where we found some Navajo jewelry that we liked. So much of the Indian jewelry that I had seen was so elaborate that one would very seldom wear it. But this piece I bought was simple enough—in a teardrop shape with the turquoise stone in the middle—that I loved to wear it and would wear it anywhere. I've enjoyed wearing it all these years. At a function recently where I wore this necklace, someone recognized the stone as coming from New Mexico. She was very knowledgeable about Indian jewelry and said to me, "I want you to know that the turquoise mine this stone came from is now closed."

Another highlight of our trip was seeing Old Faithful in Yellowstone National Park. The part that impressed me was that it really does erupt regularly, and has done so since the geyser was discovered. We have a treasure in our national parks. Did you know that for many years people have been working to preserve the natural beauty spots of America? They are trying to keep them from being commercialized. We can really see God's handiwork in these places. The effort has been put in and has resulted in a privilege that the public can enjoy now and for years to come.

We came back through Wisconsin, north of Lake Michigan, and came down through New York to Niagara Falls. While we were traveling for the six weeks, Drennan's sister, Ruth, stayed at our house.

Several weeks after we returned home, we were on a plane to California to attend Malcolm's wedding on August 1, 1987. We signed up for dance lessons because Malcolm was a very good dancer and he was marrying a very good dancer.

Milestone Anniversary

Another important event that we celebrated on the 26th of that month was our 50th wedding anniversary. We started the plans for our anniversary party the year before. Meg asked me for the names of about 72 women in my life who would be interested in embroidering a block for a quilt that would commemorate events in our lives.

Here is the note that she enclosed:

"Our parents will be celebrating their 50th wedding anniversary August 26th. We are busy making plans to celebrate the event.

We would like to give them something special that would be a keepsake from their family and friends. Mother had told us once about a 'friendship quilt' that one of her friends received. Because of her excitement in telling us about it, we thought she would appreciate and treasure one also. We are sending you a square in hopes that, as one of their friends or family you are as excited as Mother was in receiving a square to do for her friend.

We hope you will decorate the square, with washable materials, expressing something symbolic about your friendship with them or simply sign your name(s) and embroider it…The squares will be finished into a quilt and presented to them on their anniversary.

Thank you for helping us make this a special occasion for them."

Mennonite quilters cut out the blocks, which Meg mailed to women in our lives. Sixty-four blocks came back with a special memory or event embroidered on it, and each told its own story. The quilters pieced the top using the double wedding ring pattern and then quilted it. One block, which contained lace from the petticoat my mother wore on her wedding day, was made into a pillow.

Since this was a keepsake, I made up a notebook telling the story of each block. One example: a lifetime friend from Indiana made her block with a Model T Ford, and also embroidered food on one corner of it and water on another. She designed this because she rode with me as I drove the car around the farm to bring food and water to the men working there.

Another example was the telephone picture in the center with the cord leading all around the telephone. My friend, Francie, embroidered this because we talked every day on the phone. I could go on and on, but not now. Some day I hope to find the notebook that tells the story of each block.

We had a party at the Knights of Columbus here in Arlington, with 75 friends and family members attending the luncheon. When the quilt was presented, our children held it up for everyone to see. Many of the local people who had contributed a block were there. This was a wonderful occasion.

I remember John, our nephew, getting up and thanking us so much for letting them come to live with us. Many other dear people also stood to share something special. Our children also shared their reflections on our life together.

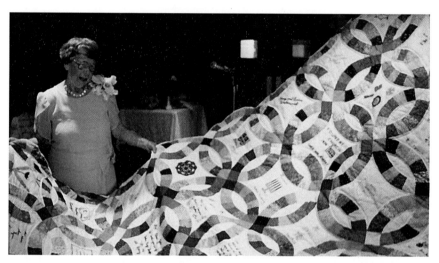

The 50ᵗʰ anniversary quilt and detail of two squares from it.

Dancing at our 50th anniversary party.

Chapter Seventeen

A Time for Everything

We were having a very quiet Christmas Day in 1989, just going to a few open houses in the neighborhood because the children wanted to have Christmas at home with their families. Drennan had mentioned on Friday that he probably was going to need a heart operation soon.

On the day after Christmas, I noticed that Drennan did not go out to bring in the newspaper as was his usual habit. I soon followed him, as he went back upstairs. He got on the phone and called the doctor's office. Then he said, "Here, take the phone," so I did. The person on the line said, "Call 911; he's having a heart attack" and I did. We were only a few blocks from the hospital, and the ambulance arrived quickly, but the paramedics were unable to stabilize Drennan right away. He was taken to Arlington Hospital, while I called Winifred, who came to get me and take me there.

After several hours, the doctor came out and said that Drennan could be kept alive, but only with help. Winifred and I looked at each other and I said, "He never wanted his life prolonged artificially." The doctor said, "Give us a few moments, and we'll come back to get you." We went to his bedside and stayed with him until he passed away. Immediately, we notified the rest of the family, and since this was Christmas vacation, they were all able to come.

We planned a small private funeral and had it at the funeral home that same week. We asked Ed Campbell to speak at the service, and he commented on Drennan's role in getting the Metrorail system started. Afterward, my beloved husband was buried at Columbia Gardens. He was 80, and we had celebrated that milestone birthday earlier in 1989 at Meg's home in Connecticut.

As we had approached our 80s, I realized that something tragic could happen to either of us at any time. I prayed that if anything should happen that it be as easy as possible. I felt that at least that prayer had been answered, and it helped me in grieving the terrible loss of my husband.

I encouraged the family to look through Drennan's closets and take home the things they felt they could use. They appreciated this offer, but it really helped me to know that they could use some of his nice clothes. The rest of his things I donated.

Our grandson Mike, who was in college at the time, accepted a gift of 40 of his grandfather's ties. He was working at a haberdashery during a vacation period from classes and was wearing one of the ties when one of his customers said to him, "I want a tie just like the one you are wearing." Mike gently explained that he had inherited his lovely silk tie from his grandfather and that there weren't any like it for sale.

Drennan and I had been scheduled to go to the Passion Play in Oberammergau, Bavaria, Germany, in the summer of 1990. Since he died before we were able to make the trip, I asked Winifred to accompany me. When I let Helga Hirsch know that we were coming, she met us in Frankfurt and went with us by boat on the Rhine River for a three-hour ride on our way to Oberammergau. It was wonderful to have her with us because she was able to show us the historical and cultural points of interest along the way.

The Passion Play was started after the Black Plague struck Europe in the 1600s. The people in Oberammergau prayed and vowed to God that they would do a Passion Play every 10 years if they would be spared and not suffer more loss than the 84 townspeople who had already died. God heard their prayers; they had no more deaths from the plague. The people kept their vow, and every 10 years since 1634 have performed a passion play—only making adjustments around the World Wars. The word "passion" here refers to the last days of Christ's life.

The little town was a quaint, quiet village where everyone who lived there participated in the play. Townspeople welcomed visitors to their homes as guests, as there were no hotels, and fed them their meals. We were fortunate to stay in the home of the man who played Joseph of Arimathea, the man who removed Jesus from the cross and placed him in his own tomb. Local crafts were available for sale, and a meal was served to the audience at the homes of their hosts during the intermission at midpoint of the eight-hour performance. The stage is out in the open, but the audience sits under cover in case of rain. The play is performed in any type of weather. Over 1,600 villagers participate without any compensation. The play is a labor of love for them.

The Passion Play stage in Oberammergau, Bavaria, Germany.

This was a two-week tour of several towns in Germany, then Geneva, Paris, and London. Two highlights of the trip were the Passion play and seeing John Wesley's home near London, England. John Wesley laid the foundation of what would become the Methodist church. He was not accepted in the Church of England so he went to America with the idea of teaching the people there. He soon felt that he was not doing what he was supposed to do, and returned to England. There he began preaching on the street corners to the working class. Later, he had his "heartwarming" experience of God. With his brother, Charles, who was a musician (and who wrote over 6,000 hymns in his lifetime), he began gathering interested Christians in small group settings, encouraging them to "Earn all you can, save all you can, and give all you can."

After Drennan died, I began to consider my life alone, and I decided that I didn't want to stay in the large two-story house on Huntington Street. We had been scheduled to move into the Jefferson retirement high-rise in Ballston when it opened, but I was not ready for a retirement home. So I considered an apartment and remembered my church friends who lived at Tower Villas. Eventually, I moved into a two-bedroom, two-bath condominium there on December 12, 1992.

I was able to sell the house on Huntington Street, but the real problem was what to do with four floors full of "things" we had accumulated over 52 years. For instance, the room above the garage had 45 years' worth of National Geographic magazines wrapped in newspaper. Only one was missing because it had Winifred's picture in it as a newborn in March 1946: They did an article on the official legal stamps to represent different certificates (birth, death, land, etc.). Because this was a complete set, with an index, I was able to donate it to an Arlington elementary school.

Another big item was Drennan's collection of United States Supreme Court decisions up to 1956. The early volumes were leatherbound. I donated the collection, appraised for $10,000, to the George Mason University Law School, which also received Drennan's collection of books on transportation and communication from the Interstate Commerce Commission.

About 1,000 books went to the McLean branch of the AAUW for its book sale. I was emptying the house piece by piece.

With the help of neighbors, I held several yard sales before condensing the contents of the house so it would fit into the much smaller apartment.

I finally cleared out the house on January 28, 1993, bringing the last few boxes of belongings to the new apartment.

In 1993, Winifred's physician, without taking a biopsy, told her a lump in her breast was benign. A year later, the lump became painful, and cancer had spread to her lymph nodes. Despite chemotherapy, she died August 12, 1994.

If I had known at the time, I would have insisted that she have a second opinion. She said later, "Either God's going to heal me, or I'm ready to go." And, "It's better to have lived a short time than a long time and suffer."

We never know how long our path is here on Earth. Winifred's ended too soon, and even today I find her passing too sad to address at length here.

I did need to continue with my life, however, and today I feel so blessed that I made a decision to get out of the house while I was still able to do it. It took me two years, but that has been worth it.

I think deciding to get out of the big house was one of the smartest things I ever did. I was not stuck there with all of its contents when I got too frail to move all of it myself. Too many people stay in their house too long, and then moving becomes a burden for their family.

I've been so blessed by living at Tower Villas. It's close to my church, and people have been very generous about picking me up and giving me rides. It has helped me become more active in the church, leading to my four years as president of the United Methodist Women during the 1990s.

I eventually gave Meg the English mahogany drop-leaf table with wooden hinges because I knew she would care for it like the museum piece it is.

The Holy Land

By 1994, I was settled in at Tower Villas and very active in my church, so I decided to take a trip to the Holy Land with our pastor, the Rev. Robert Stamps and his wife Ellen. It was eventful and tragic, since the leader of Israel was assassinated during our visit.

We departed on October 31, 1995, on a TWA flight to Tel Aviv. On our first morning we boarded a boat, crossed the Sea of Galilee, and visited a museum containing the remains of a wooden boat found in the sea that is cited in several biblical passages as one from which Jesus had his disciples cast fishing nets. We visited the well where Jesus spoke to the woman sitting at the well, the amphitheatre where David was thrown to the lions, the Dome of the Rock, Dome of Spirit, Mount of Olives, the site of the crucifixion, the Wailing Wall, the Dead Sea, the Holy Sepulchre Church, King David's tomb, the spot where Jesus preached the sermon on the mount, Nazareth, Mount Carmel, Bethlehem, and the Jordan River, where I reaffirmed my baptism. In the midst of our visit, an assassin killed Prime Minister Yitzhak Rabin with gunshots on November 4, 1995, as Rabin was departing a rally at city hall in Tel Aviv in support of the Oslo Accords, which created the Palestinian Authority, gave it land in Gaza and on the West Bank, and could have led to the creation of a nation of Palestine. Rabin, Shimon Peres and Yasser Arafat had been awarded the Nobel Peace Prize for the accords, but while many Israelis welcomed the promise of peace the accords would bring, many others did not. Yigal Amir, Rabin's assassin, vehemently opposed the Oslo agreement. Two days later, sirens sounded for Rabin's funeral and all activity ceased. After the funeral, we visited the Upper Room, where Jesus had his last supper with his disciples.

As we prepared to depart Israel, Bob Stamps commented that it would be nice to have a couple more days. We boarded the plane, which had not fully refueled because of high winds and headed for Madrid, where we were to refuel again before taking off for America. Soon after the plane departed Madrid, the left engine caught fire, and the pilot headed back to a landing in Madrid. The passengers were either in our group or in a group of Mennonites, and I felt that everyone aboard was praying for a safe landing. It was a scary moment for all of us. The pilot brought the plane down, and it felt to me as though the plane were being gently settled on the ground. The Spanish airlines were on strike, so we had to stay in Madrid until a new engine was flown in, installed and tested on our TWA jetliner. This took two days, but the bonus was that we were treated royally and were able to make an unanticipated visit to beautiful Toledo.

Footsteps of the Apostle Paul

In 1997, I made a second journey with the Rev. Stamps

and his wife, this time in a group that followed the footsteps of the Apostle Paul in Greece. In Athens, we visited the Acropolis, the market, the Temple of Zeus and other sites before heading to Corinth, where Paul had founded a church, and Philippi, where he baptized his first European convert. Other remarkable stops were ancient monasteries, Thessaloniki, Delphi, and the Temple of Apollo. Along the way, there were marvelous views of Mount Olympus and miles of olive groves. Part of the journey was aboard a ship that took us to Mykonos and its white-washed houses. From there we sailed to Turkey, where a bus took us to Ephesus, a key city in ancient Asia Minor. Then it was on to the island of Patmos, where John wrote the book of Revelations, to Rhodes and the Temple of Athena, and to Santorini and Crete.

I had the great fun of having my grandson David live with me for a year and a half after he graduated from Rochester Institute of Technology in the mid-1990s. But David said it was embarrassing to admit to a date that he lived with his grandmother, so eventually he and a friend rented an apartment on their own. Having him here gave me the rare opportunity to get to know my oldest grandson very well.

I gave a dinner for a friend who had gotten engaged and invited a young lady from my church to round out the table. David disapproved, so my only attempt at matchmaking was not appreciated.

On September 11, 2001, about 8:30 a.m., the World Trade Center in New York City was hit by a plane that burst into flames. Then, about 20 minutes later, the second tower of the center was hit by a second plane, which also exploded in flames. A bit later, a third plane hit the Pentagon building in Arlington, where the military people work. A fourth hijacked plane crashed in Pennsylvania. This was definitely a "terrorist attack" on the United States of America. More than 2,500 people died in these events, and the country was in a state of shock. Immediately, everyone began to ask who could have done such a terrible thing as this.

Within a week, the government had good reasons to believe that these events were planned and carried out by the same terrorist group that had committed other terrorist activities in New York previously and in other parts of the world: Al Qaeda led by Osama bin Laden. History will record many details about that week, but I will leave that to the history writers. My thoughts are: I am very sad and mourn with the families that lost loved ones. Our economic system is challenged, and the stock market has gone down. Our security system will be strengthened. And in the long run, the United States will get back to normal and be a free country where we can continue to live at peace with each other and the rest of the world.

Time Out

Here I want to share that I stopped writing on my autobiography because of health issues. Just to summarize a bit, here is what happened: In the year 2000 I was in the hospital, unconscious, for 2½ weeks due to low sodium. My electrolytes were very low. I spent time in the rehab center trying to get my strength back, so I did not get back to my writing during that time.

Although I was in a coma, I had many vivid dreams, some related to my treatment and some pure fantasies. In one, I dreamed I was a wonderful singer preparing to give a concert in a park. The next day I asked if the newspaper had written about it, but it hadn't. All part of the dream. Meg revealed later that she had been playing tapes of Irish music in an effort to ease me out of the coma, so that may have sparked my imagination.

Another time I dreamed I was rolling down a slope in a wheelchair and couldn't get my hands together or stop the wheelchair. The dream ended. Later I found that my hands really were tied to a wheelchair to prevent me from removing the IV from my arm.

I had visitors while in the coma, but I didn't recall any of them though I am grateful for their wishes and prayers.

My daughter told me that they thought they were going to lose me, and the family was concerned that my doctor might not have done everything in her power to help me. After I recovered, I related this to the doctor, and said, "Now, I'd like to hear your side of the story."

"Well," said Dr. Kong, "I could have given you a certain medicine, but it might have affected your memory."

She had no notion that I was in the process of putting together this book. I see this as another instance of God's help in my life.

In 2002, I was beginning to have pain in my back and hips that was later diagnosed as a pinched sciatic nerve. As treatment for this pain, I was scheduled to take a series of shots in my back, but these did not help my pain. Finally the doctor sent me to a bone specialist named Dr. Evans. After having my hip x-rayed, I was told that my hip bones were rubbing against each other, and that I needed to have my hip replaced. "I will take care of your hip pain but not the rest of the pain," he said.

In the spring of 2003, I underwent hip-replacement surgery followed by weeks of physical therapy. It was a joy to find that the pain in my back and hip were gone!

In the year 2004, when I was 94, I began to have trouble seeing. I'd known for many years that I had the beginning of macular degeneration but never once thought that it would ever cause me any trouble. Dr. Cupples, a retina specialist, examined my eyes when I noticed that I could not see as well as usual. He said that my macular degeneration had changed to the wet kind. This meant the blood vessels in the back of my eye had started to seep blood. When this happens, the eye can be treated, which the doctor did.

After about a year and a half, both eyes were treated, and I am now considered to be legally blind and cannot drive. But doctors have not found a way to bring the eyesight back to normal, so now I can say that "I'm conveniently blind" because my home-care insurance allows me to have help five days a week to do the things I can't see to do, such as reading recipes, cleaning, keeping my clothes clean, and so forth.

In 2005 at the age of 95, I bought a sight machine, a new computer, and a new program called Zoom Text that made it possible for me to read e-mail and dictate to the computer as it types what I am saying.

In early 2011, I had another major surgery that took me away from writing for more than a year. Now, at age 101, I'm feeling much better than I did a year ago and try to walk at least ¼ mile every day in the hallways of Tower Villas. God again has blessed me with good health, a wonderful memory, and a joy of living! So now, I'm working on completing my autobiography.

Return to Purdue

Even though every day holds special moments for me, one of my outstanding experiences this century was my return to Purdue University for the 73ʳᵈ annual Christmas music program in 2006.

Ellen Stamps, with whom I had traveled to the Holy Land and Greece, asked me to accompany her to West Lafayette. Ellen and her friend Betsy Marti had arranged for me to be recognized during intermission as the oldest Purdue alumna in attendance, which was a great surprise, honor and joy for me. Other alumni were helping to lead the singing, and I stood with them on stage as they and the 6,000 members of the audience sang Christmas carols.

I had attended the first Purdue Christmas concert when I was a junior in 1933. Over the years, the programs grew, and in 2006 performances were given seven times over the first weekend in December with more than 120 people taking part and about 42,000 people in the live audiences. The productions often are televised nationally around Christmas Eve.

The theme in 2006 was "Christmas Is Believing," and the director said, "If everyone here has enough faith, it just might snow." It wasn't long before "snow" began falling on the stage.

Chapter Eighteen

The Celebration of a Century

The first thought I had about my 100ᵗʰ birthday was that I didn't want it to be focused just on me. Meg and I talked about different possibilities to carry out my desire. I wanted events be enjoyable for my family, the church, and my many other friends.

We soon came up with the idea of having two events: a catered dinner for family and relatives on Saturday evening, which was my real birthday date, and a reception on Sunday afternoon at the church. Then there was the question of how all of this would get done.

Early on, Meg volunteered to do the decorating and the invitations for both events. The timing was important because out-of-town guests and relatives would need to buy plane tickets and reserve rooms at a hotel. Meg and Phil had plans to be in Italy for six weeks during May and the first part of June. This meant the invitations needed to be ready to mail before they left. I offered to help by getting the names and addresses on labels for Meg to use to mail them.

It was also my job to think about and plan the reception for my friends, and the catered dinner for the family and relatives. Needless to say, I felt the need of some help! I didn't expect the women of the church to take on the responsibility of the reception without some incentive. My idea was that if I could find someone to take on the planning of all the details of the reception, it would make it much easier for me. I immediately thought of asking my friend, Pam Gibert, because she had demonstrated that she was quite an organizer and capable of planning such a reception. I went to her and explained my idea; she happily accepted. This was the first of many blessings that I received during the planning of the celebration. I felt so blessed because I knew that she would do a very good job.

I told Pam my plan: I would pay for all the food and beverages, and would give a sizeable donation to the church for the time and effort of those involved. Then we discussed who else should be asked to help. Trudy Ensign and Dee Culver, longtime church members, became a part of the project.

I immediately called the church secretary to make sure that the social hall was available for the August 6th weekend.

Pam began to plan the reception. I had told her that Meg would be interested in helping as things developed. In Pam's planning, she communicated with Meg and me to work in our wishes. After a time, Pam gave me a typed sheet of the plan that she and her committee had decided to pursue. She sent one to Meg, too. I could now relax about the reception!

Now my attention could be turned to finding the best hotel rates for my guests and a caterer for the dinner on Saturday. I first had to find the best rates so that that information could be put on the invitations. When I told the local Hilton that this was a celebration for a 100th birthday, they immediately became more interested. The representative checked with her supervisor and they gave me a special rate on the rooms of $69/night. I had called several other places and the rates were more than the Hilton's offer; it also occurred to me that the Hilton might be able to cater. I decided to go there. Then, I checked with Meg and Phil, who travel a lot, about the food at the Hilton: was it good? They thought the food was great, so I felt good about talking with the Hilton to provide the celebration meal on Saturday.

Meg and I spoke with A'Lyce, the catering sales manager, about a menu. There were two different prices: $34/plate for no choice on the entrée; $37/plate with a choice. We decided to offer a choice of chicken or beef, and could now put that information on the invitations.

I had originally planned to have the catered dinner in the social hall on Saturday evening. It was all working out for the best: When we moved it to the Hilton, that alleviated a lot of stress because the Sunday reception could be set up at the church the evening before.

Earlier, Meg had created an e-mail account to receive the RSVPs for both the dinner and the reception. She was going to mail two special invitations that she had created herself: one for the dinner for family and relatives, and one for the open-house reception. In both cases, the guests were to respond to the Gmail address that Meg monitored.

I didn't know it, but the head chef at the Hilton was talking with Meg about the menu and had asked her if she could come in for a tasting. Meg lived too far away and was on her way out of town so she had to refuse, but she suggested that her mother might love to do this. He told her that he would make a special lunch for me and a guest.

Since Meg wanted to make this a surprise for me, she called my friend, Marci Schiller, and suggested that she be the person to go along with me to the tasting. Marci quickly admitted to me that she would not be the best person for the adventure because she was allergic to anything with flour in it! As things developed, I had the knowledge of the appointment, but I didn't know everything that would unfold.

Some time later, I arranged to have the tasting at the Hilton, and decided to take Pam along with me, who was a wonderful connoisseur of food and flavors.

When Pam started planning, she asked me if I had a biography! I told her no, but I could arrange to have one made. My nephew, John Allen, who had lived with us for seven years when he was a child, and Jo, his wife, were now both retired from working at the Washington Post. They still lived nearby. I immediately thought that John and his wife were the logical ones to ask to do the biography for my 100th celebration.

I called them and asked if they'd be interested in a little project. They accepted the challenge, and a few days later, they were over at my condo, John with his laptop and Jo with her pencil and pad. They spent several hours listening to me review the highlights of my life.

As it turned out, Jo took this on as a publicity extravaganza! She did things that I never expected: she contacted both the Washington Post and the Sun Gazette for picture-taking and interviews. Besides designing and typing up a beautiful biography, she made enough copies to hand out at my celebrations, and probably some left to send to those who weren't able to attend.

Pam asked another question: "Are you going to have music, or pictures?" I knew exactly who to ask regarding the pictures: J. Paul Lewis, from my church. I knew he would do a great job because I had attended the Sunday evening services for several years where he was responsible for projecting the pictures on the wall that corresponded so beautifully with the music we sang. He quickly responded yes—another blessing— and came to my condo to scan pictures onto a computer to use in the social hall at the church during the reception.

Midway between the planning and the event, Paul and his wife, Laura, had a big fire at their home. The computer with all of the pictures stored in it had been lost and would not be available for my reception. My first thought was concern for their safety, and finding out that Paul and Laura were going to be all right was a relief. I accepted the fact that we just would not have any pictures for the reception.

In talking later, Paul indicated that he would scan the pictures over once he got his new equipment. "Paul, we don't have to have those," I told him. "You must have plenty of things that need doing." But as soon as Paul got the equipment replaced, he came back over to rescan the photos; the new equipment scanned the pictures even better. Another blessing! How the Lord provides!

Soon it was time for the special luncheon with the Hilton chef. The plan was to have little samplings of the food prepared as it would be for the dinner. When we arrived at the Hilton, they parked the car for us. A'Lyce came down to meet us and introduce us to Chef Jeff Gentry. In a lovely, little, private section of the dining room we were served the different examples that we had talked about. In choosing the menu I wanted it to be something that sounded special; the starch was to be mashed potatoes or rice. The rice was very special: it was light and creamy, almost like mashed potatoes. I chose that for both entrees.

When it came to the meat, he served grilled chicken with mango salsa, and it really was the best chicken I've ever eaten.

Pam and I thought we would have a 90-minute lunchtime tasting of his recipes; it turned into three hours! The special rice, which I found out later was risotto, went just as well with the beef entrée as it had the chicken. I tasted everything that he offered us and decided on the Saturday meal: five assortments of breads, salad, asparagus on the side, both the beef and chicken entrees, coffee, tea, and dessert: some birthday cake and a serving of sherbet.

At the end of our time together, Chef Jeff surprised me by saying that the Hilton was going to give me my birthday cake for the dinner at no charge!

During much of this time, I was recuperating from major surgery that occurred on February 14th. However, I was having fun enjoying how things were going for my 100th birthday. My only other responsibility was to okay the plans as different people were sharing them with me. I hope you have the sense of how much I was enjoying how the plans were unfolding for this special occasion.

Meg arrived back in South Carolina from Italy on Tuesday, June 14, and on Wednesday she landed here to participate with me in the National AAUW Convention on Thursday, which was being held in Washington, D.C. She stayed a week. We were to be at the Renaissance Hotel by 1 p.m. so that I could be introduced as the oldest active member of the organization. After the introduction, I was invited to go to a soundproof room where I was interviewed on video that was put on the national website. During that interview I was asked about the important AAUW events in my life. As of this writing, I have been a member for 68 years.

A bit of historical information: The founding mothers of AAUW in the late 1870s discovered that their educations did not guarantee them employment. They decided that they should band together and work for equity. AAUW has been working for equity for women this whole time. You might recall that at that time in our nation's history, women could not even vote.

Sue Zajac, a dear friend in AAUW, offered to make a cake for the reception. It seemed like too much for her to do this, so at first I said, "No." After some thought, I called her back and said, "Sue, if you'd really like to do it, then I accept, especially since I remembered that you did my 90th birthday cake, too!" She suggested that she make three cakes to form the number 100.

Sue Zajac baked three different recipes for my special 100th birthday cakes.

Some special events happened before my big day.

A few weeks beforehand, I had received greetings from the President and First Lady of the United States, a birthday letter from the Governor of Virginia, a commendation each from the Senate and the House of Delegates of the Commonwealth of Virginia, a proclamation from the Arlington County Board, and a recognition from the Ballston-Virginia Square Civic Association. Dear Jo Allen had each one framed for display.

Then, on Friday, July 29, I was interviewed by the local paper, the Sun Gazette.

On Wednesday, August 3, on my way to get my hair done, I shared with the taxi driver that I was almost 100 years old, and he insisted on giving me my ride for free! The hairdresser also would not take payment for her work; Mabel Bailey has been doing my hair for close to 20 years. I was exhilarated that so many people were celebrating me! Mabel asked if Norma Cunningham, who shampoos my hair, could come to the reception too. Norma had so much fun telling her friends and neighbors that she was going to a party for someone who was going to be 100 that I was happy to include her.

I came home to meet with the Washington Post reporter whom Jo had arranged to interview me. In the middle of our conversation, Meg and Phil arrived from South Carolina. The reporter took several photographs and then suggested that Meg join me on the davenport. That's the one the editors used with his article. Malcolm arrived later that evening from California.

That evening, we had a quick supper before going downstairs to a party in the lobby of my building, Tower Villas. About a week or 10 days before the party, the condominium's Social Committee announced that it was celebrating my 100th birthday, and posted an invitation at the front desk, as well as putting one in each resident's mailbox. After that, people were soon asking at the desk: Who is she? Do I know her? Where does she live?

So, the woman at the desk asked me to bring down a picture that she could post with the invitation, which I did.

I decided ahead of time that I was really going to dress up for this occasion at Tower Villas because turning 100 only happens once in a lifetime. This was my first party, three days away from my actual birthday. I looked through my closet and chose a beautiful aqua formal dress that I had worn several times at events that had taken place when Drennan was serving in the federal government. I had lost some weight and was able to fit back into it. Many years ago, I decorated it with a braid of sparkles from one of Shirley MacLaine's old dresses I had bought at a second-hand store. Her parents, the Beattys, had been our neighbors on Huntington Street.

At the Tower Villas reception.

When my family and I got downstairs, I sat down in a chair that was being saved for me. The Social Committee brought out a wrist corsage for me to wear. Everyone was having a wonderful time. Later, we had cake and sparkling cider. When it was time for the toast, they made sure each one had something to drink to raise a glass.

Jo and John Allen were invited to come to this party, and Jo brought along copies of the biography to hand out to anyone who wanted one. Even after the gathering, anyone who expressed regret about not being able to attend was offered a biography.

There were many who were so complimentary; after they were done speaking, I asked to have a chance to address the group and expressed my appreciation for the celebration. People gradually went home, and about 10 p.m., we headed back upstairs.

Meg and I talked ahead of time about how we were going to feed the immediate family during that weekend. I gave her the name and telephone number of Ann Godfrey, a retired teacher who took up catering. They arranged for meals. Meg decided that anyone who could come to the Friday evening meal should. Phil picked up a cake so that we could celebrate the other August and September birthdays in the family while we were together.

As the family began to gather, we had six for dinner on Thursday, and 17 on Friday! With the catered food we had arranged to bring in—plus some additional salads—we got to visit and feast together.

On Saturday our main focus was the sit-down dinner for the relatives at the Hilton; there were 30 of us. Arthur's youngest son was hiking in the Alps hours before the family gathered together. He made it in time for the dinner, which he promised he would, then flew out at 4 a.m. the next day to get home to Madison, Wisconsin, to meet his son, who was coming for a visit. That's devotion to carrying through on a promise!

The dinner at the Hilton was at 6 p.m.; the family was invited to meet at 5 p.m. in a room next to the dining area where I had asked for enough chairs for each one to sit and visit before the dinner started.

Since Meg is so artistic, she was able to take 100 roses in varying shades of pink, and make them into beautiful arrangements for the tables. She managed to get it all done in the small space of my back bathroom! She had also placed pink balloons and napkins on the tables with the flowers. We reused the decorations the next afternoon at the church.

I was disappointed that more relatives could not come due to age and infirmities, but we had a pleasant if small family reunion that was very enjoyable. Eventually, I shared copies of the biography and of the newspaper interviews with my nephews and their families who were unable to attend so that they could share in my joys. One of them responded with a letter, written in someone else's hand, so I knew it would have been impossible for him to travel.

Granddaughter Annette Filiatrault, left, and daughter Meg Filiatrault, right, with me at the family dinner.

The family dinner guests, from left to right. Front row: Makaela Riggs, Charles Filiatrault, Henry Filiatrault, Ben Filiatrault, Camron Riggs. Middle row: Adrienne Leo, Elaine Leo, Annette Filiatrault, Malcolm Robert Miller, Martha Ann Miller, Margaret "Meg" Filiatrault, Lee Riggs, John Riggs, Chanda Riggs. Back row: Katrina Filiatrault, Michael Filiatrault, Jo Allen, John Allen, Summer Adams, David Filiatrault, Carol Riggs, Brian Payne, Christine Colby, Alex Colby, Brian Riggs, Phil Filiatrault.

Dinner was a very relaxed time: We went from table to table just visiting with one another and enjoying being together. I went to every table and sat with each party for a little while; it was a joy to reminisce. The children behaved wonderfully because a thoughtful relative, Mike's wife, Katrina, brought toys along for them to play with while the adults visited.

As promised, the hotel furnished the cake for free. And how beautifully decorated it was! While we ate the dessert, we had a time of toasting, with everyone having a chance to speak if they wanted. Both Meg and Malcolm had comments to make, and thanked people for being there. Various others got up and shared who they were, how far they had come, and wishes for my future.

It was so convenient to have all of the family in one location for lodging. Meg, Phil, and I were the only ones who had to travel after the dinner broke up around nine. The Hilton even furnished free parking for the car that brought me to the hotel. Although they often handle weddings and big parties, they told me that they seldom had an opportunity to host a 100th birthday celebration, so they bent over backwards to make this a wonderful occasion. The Hilton helped to make my birthday very special.

We went to bed pretty quickly. It was decided that since we had the reception at the church in the afternoon, we wouldn't try to go to services in the morning. They had cancelled the social hour following the 11 a.m. service to encourage people to leave right away so that they could come back to enjoy my reception at 4 p.m. It was nice to be relaxed in the morning and not try to fit too much in.

It was to be an open house type of reception that would go from 4 to 7 p.m.; I was ready to leave for the church by 2. I decided that since Meg was using pink in the balloons and flowers that I would just wear my light pink sheath dress with a full-length pink French lace coat that I had made for a grandson's August wedding several years before.

The key event of the celebrating was the reception at the church. Pam had planned the event so carefully that 22 people were helping around the room at special stations: at the beverage table, the food tables, the guest book, the sign-up sheet for those interested in knowing when this book is published. There was even someone assigned to direct people to parking spaces, and there were greeters at the door. I so appreciated those who were busy in the kitchen and didn't have much time to visit because of the necessary service that they provided.

We tried to make things as easy as possible for the food preparation of the heavy hors d'oeuvres. As an example, we used filet mignon that was easily sliced and placed into the wonderful small rolls from Heidelberg Bakery for sandwiches.

Pam had purchased trays of food (cheese plates, fruit platters, veggie trays) and various other things that were on the menu. I didn't get to eat very much as I was busy greeting all of my guests! The room was arranged in such a way that the flow of people was very smooth: The cake table was in front of the stage, and three rows of food tables ran perpendicular to it, but they were arranged in such a way that they didn't block movement from the front of the hall to the back.

I was given a seat opposite the food tables with a chair on each side of me for guests to sit on and be comfortable as they had a turn wishing me well. There were other activities going on at the same time: people taking pictures, lots of visiting and enjoying the wonderful slide show of scanned photos, and, of course, eating. There was plenty of food left over.

Since there were many people from the AAUW group that came to the reception, one of its past presidents got us all together to pose for a picture of that special group.

Photo by J. Paul Lewis

My friends from AAUW celebrated my birthday with me. From left, are, seated, Marjorie Hobart, Branch Past President; Caroline Pickens, AAUW of Virginia President; me; Nancy Joyner, Northern District Co-representative; Winnie Macfarlan, and Doris Moore. Standing are Karen Darner, Chrystia Sonevytsky, Susan Zajac, Arlington County Board Vice President Mary Hynes, and Michele Milden, Branch Past President.

Many guests signed the border of an amusing poster that Beth Lewis, Reilly's wife, had made for me from a silly photo she had taken and doctored.

Photo and design by Beth Lewis

At 5 p.m., Meg, who was the hostess, called everyone's attention to a short program she had arranged. She had listed this in the invitations so that anyone who wanted to be there for this part of the reception could be.

One of the special speakers was Arlington County Board Chairman Chris Zimmerman. He read a copy of a proclamation that emphasized many of the major events of my life in relation to Arlington County, including the time that I was recognized with a Person of Vision award by the County's Commission on the Status of Women in 1997.

At the very end of the gathering, when Meg was thanking everyone and saying our goodbyes, there was suddenly the sound of thunder. I didn't know it at the time, but there was heavy rain off and on during the event.

Meg spontaneously said, "Even the Heavens are clapping for Mother's birthday!"

That was the one thing that many people mentioned to me about their memory of the reception.

I couldn't believe that so many came out in the rain: 200 people showed up in spite of the weather! We had such a wonderful time. I had spoken briefly with our church treasurer, Cecil Corry, weeks before this celebration, and he had said to me, "This will probably be the biggest birthday celebration that we've had at the church that I can remember." (Cecil had become a member of Clarendon more than 60 years earlier.) So many of our church members have lived to 100, but have not been healthy or mobile enough to come to the church to be celebrated. We lost Cecil only a week before this event; I hope he was enjoying it from his new home.

Escorted by my son Malcolm Miller, left, and my grandson Mike Filiatrault, I prepared to blow out the candles on my cakes.

In looking back at the whole event, it went far beyond my expectations because of the love that was shared, along with so many people showing how much they cared. It happened just as I'd hoped: We were able to have an event that seemed to be fun for many people.

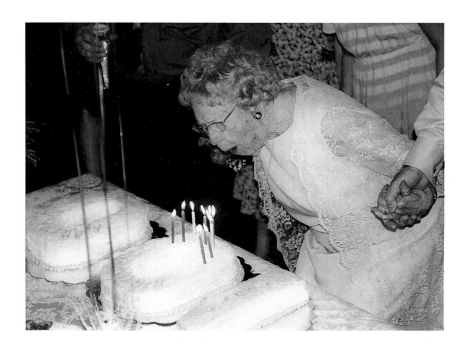

The 100th birthday candles were close enough together that I could extinguish them with one breath.

Along with all the rest of the celebrating that I've shared here, I received in the mail, or by personal contact, 140 greeting cards, one of which was the largest greeting card I've ever been given. It was partially hand-painted and was sent from my friend Helga Hirsch in Germany.

There were so many mini-celebrations that happened, too. I kept receiving cards and well-wishes from far and near. These other unique things happened after my birthday lunch:

August 15: A luncheon with friends.

August 19: My Tower Villas neighbor Tom Cayhill, who had been promising me for more than two years that he would have Willard Scott announce my 100th birthday on the "Today" show, phoned to say that everything was going according to plan. I had not taken Tom seriously, though I was flattered by his suggestion and intrigued by the possibility of getting nationwide recognition for my milestone.

Once during the year prior, I said to him, "Oh, come on,

Tom, quit kidding me. They tell me it takes three years to get on his show to have it announced."

"Oh, not me," he assured me, "I'm a special friend of his!" Indeed, many years earlier, Willard Scott did live in Arlington County, and they probably did know each other. I decided to wait and see if he could come through with his promise.

When he called to say I would be recognized on television the very next day, I called Meg and Phil right away. Tom came to my condo and set my tv to the correct channel. The next morning, Willard Scott announced my name on the "Today" show while my picture moved across the screen.

August 23: My first experience with an earthquake. I stood up and looked over at the dining room table and saw the chandelier swinging back and forth. A couple of the plaques that were sitting on the table fell over, but no damage occurred. Imagine being 100 years old and never having experienced an earthquake. I said, "This is an earthquake; what do I do? What do I do now?!" By then, the earthquake was over. Very short, thank goodness! After it was over I was glad that it had happened so that I knew what an earthquake was like. One is never too old to experience something new, even an earthquake. I wondered what the world was trying to tell us.

August 27: Then, within a week, Hurricane Irene was coming up the East Coast, and we prepared as we were advised to do in case the electricity went off for a period of time. Fortunately, the hurricane did not come that far into the Northern Virginia area. Now that it's all over, I'm happy to report that we didn't lose electricity for a moment!

Finally, a couple of things that happened in September wound up the planned celebrations by others:

September 20: AAUW well-wishing with another birthday cake!

September 23: I am now a member of the 10^2 (ten-squared) Club of The Library of Congress. One day at church, Pete Davis was explaining how the National Book Service for the Blind and Handicapped, which provides talking book services that I use, was interested in recognizing my 100th birthday. I then received an official letter explaining the time and place to be for the ceremony. Pete and his wife, Lottie, picked me up and took me to the event at the Arlington Central Library. In the letter announcing the occasion, they had suggested that I invite a few friends to come and be with me. The small room was filled with people from the staff and friends from church. They presented me with a pretty circular pin, and a certificate that I am now a 10^2 Talking-Book Club Member. This is an exclusive club for centenarians; there are three of us in Arlington County.

October 2: The final capping of the continued celebrations: My friend and lawyer, Jack Melnick, gave me a framed historical record of House Bill No. 29 from 1976 that he offered with three others when he was a member of the Virginia House of Delegates. Had this bill passed, it would have repealed the post-integration law that prohibited Arlington voters from electing their school board.

After this happened, and I was sure that everything had taken place, I received a box in the mail. On the inside was a postcard that read, "Happy Birthday from Your Friends at Smucker's" and inside were 12 one-ounce jars of their jams: apricot, strawberry and orange marmalade. I was so surprised, from Orrville, Ohio, I figured my friend Amy Barr, who grew up in Ohio, would know something about it.

She was very knowledgeable about the company and told me that Willard Scott's program is sponsored by the Smucker's company! She also revealed that she and my grandson, David, worked to get the picture that was used on August 19 to announce my 100th birthday on Willard Scott's television segment. Another blessing!

Chapter Nineteen

Wisdom

Even though I am "not ready for the rocking chair yet," I must bring this book to a close.

As a child I always enjoyed looking at a picture that was in our parlor, and I've had it in my home all my life.

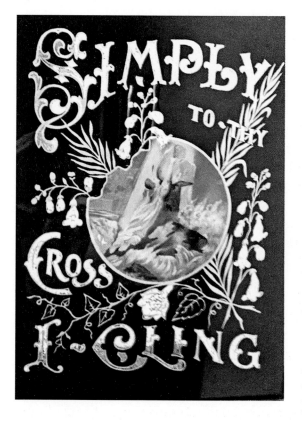

I like to think of the cross as having two parts: a vertical, and a horizontal, line. The vertical line represents our relationship with God; the horizontal line is our relationships with others. You don't have a cross until you put the two parts together.

Our relationship with God should help us make decisions in our relationships with each other. In living, people sometimes make bad decisions. But, if it's always done in relationship to Jesus' teachings in life, then we're on a path to spiritual maturity.

God sent Jesus to Earth to teach us about our human relationships. Jesus also allows us to decide whether we will follow Him, or not. So if we accept Jesus Christ down deep in our hearts as our Savior, and truly do try to live a humble life, we will know the real joys of living.

As we follow Him, our spiritual lives are maturing. The joys of trying to live a Christian life become more evident the older we get, which leads to a peace of mind: "Thy will be done, O God, not mine." I've reached a point in my life in which I feel a peace of mind that I'm not afraid of dying, or what's to come, that whatever happens will be all right.

By clinging to the cross, we can have a positive approach to life. Otherwise, we can get depressed very easily as human beings. I hope you can see that it's "to Thy cross I cling." God has been my guiding light, and I give God credit for what and where I am today.

I believe that the most important thing that has ever been recorded in history is that God sent Jesus to Earth to teach us how to live. God took the cruelty of the cross and changed it to a symbol of hope and promise.

The first blessing of my life was that I was fortunate to be born into a Christian family; for this I have always been grateful. My mother and father were always examples of good values in life.

We never worked on Sunday except for the chores that had to be done every day, such as milking the cows. We always went to church every Sunday, not because we had to but because we wanted to. This helped us to know what was going on in the community, but more important, to study the Word of God and the Bible.

I don't want to leave the impression that life is easy, and that one doesn't face problems. With a positive attitude, one can face any situation with God's help.

As I was approaching my 100th year, people asked me, "How did you do it?" referring to my good health and ability to walk around and enjoy life. First of all, God gave us a special body within which to live—the only one we will ever have—so we must take care of it. Study the beautiful machine that we are; its needs are very special. And care for it by eating correctly. One thing that has helped me not to have any pain has been to take Super Vitamin B Complex Plus C. How we feel is very important as we travel life's journey. We should always remember our actions speak louder than words.

Now I am going to make a few comments regarding our horizontal relating and share some of the gems that I have enjoyed through my life. To do more would take another book.

Good Steward of Money

When we have money to spend, we should think carefully about how to spend it. We talked about it before we were married, and that we would never spend more money than we had to live on. That meant setting up a budget. When you plan a budget, you take into consideration all you expect to spend in a month's time. The first part should be God's part, and the next part should be something put away for the future. Then estimate what each thing in your life is going to cost, like clothes, food, shelter and so forth. It isn't how much we make, but what we do with what we make that is good for the budget.

For example, when we made our first budget after we were married with his $198 monthly government salary, all that was left for recreation was a $1.50 per month for both of us. We would go walking instead of buying something.

Another thing about a budget: Never start borrowing from one item and use it for another item. This meant that when we had taxes to pay, we had the money. Therefore, we didn't have to wonder where it was coming from. Because I liked figures, I liked doing this, but not enjoying the process should not keep one from having a budget. At times, I even told the children that we did not have the money for a new dress or another pair of shoes. I think that they sometimes thought I was lying, because their response would be, "Well, we have money for everything else." I was then able to point out to them that that money was set aside for food or shelter, and one should not spend that designated money on clothes.

As a result, I'm living life with money to take care of myself in a comfortable fashion.

As money relates to marriage, we never argued or fussed over money: He knew exactly where it was going and why. Our relationships were more peaceful and calm because we were in harmony over those things. As his salary increased, our budget changed.

Good Steward of Time

In the same way, we tried to be good stewards of our time. In this light, we decide: If church is important to us, then we go to church.

How we spend our time enters into everything in life. Is God in your plan for the spending of your time? That influences how you spend it. In our lives, we found it very important to spend our time working for better schools. In so doing, we have helped thousands of children by working for good schools until we got them.

Honesty Always Pays

I believe that honesty always pays. I had been at the store, and after returning home, discovered that I had too much money in my pocketbook. It was really because of my budget that I knew this, because of the record-keeping habits I had. I loaded the children back into the car to go to the store again. The children may not have remembered, but the clerk was very grateful.

Another example of honesty is when I was audited one year. They didn't find a cent wrong, just numbers that were put together instead of separate. I was audited the next year, and they didn't find a cent I hadn't reported. But the feeling that I had was, "Well, it pays to be honest." I didn't have to lie about anything. One lie tends to bring on other lies to cover up the first lie.

Joy of Serving Others

When I returned to Indiana to visit friends and family, I would have lunch with Alice and Bernice—life-long friends from grade school. Often, Alice would have me spend the night at her home on my trips. One time, when we were back at Alice's after lunch, we commented that Bernice really needed a new set of teeth: We had observed them dropping down into her mouth when she ate, which was a little unpleasant to see. I said, "Alice, do you think that we could help Bernice with getting some proper teeth? She probably doesn't have the money for it, so she hasn't gotten it done." Alice's comment was that she didn't think she would be able to speak to Bernice about it, but she knew that her dentist, who was a wonderful person, might be able to help, and she would speak to him about it.

So, I approached Bernice and said, "Bernice, what I am going to say to you is said in Christian love." I went on to say that we would pay for a set of teeth if she would go to Alice's dentist and get the work done. When I talked with her, she was very receptive to the idea. I know for a fact that she had spent what money she had on her sister and other people instead of taking care of her own needs.

From this point forward, Alice made arrangements with her dentist, and Bernice kept the appointments. It turned out that the dentist, as a child, had gone to the library many times and had heard Bernice, who was the librarian, give the story hour to the children. I felt that because he had enjoyed her stories at the library, he bent over backward to do a really special thing for her.

To make a long story short, he did far more than just making a set of teeth: He had to operate as well. Since I was sharing half of the expense, I'm sure the doctor did not charge what he usually did for the needs of this patient. She was so appreciative that she gave Alice and me each an angel—in her words a "tooth fairy"—sitting on a basket that contained a thank you note.

It is a joy to serve others, and this went beyond anything I ever dreamed as a possibility.

Hospitality

After buying a house that had room for meetings, we always invited people to come in. Later on, people said I was always very hospitable by opening my house to so many groups. I had never dreamed of having a home in that neighborhood because I thought the houses were more expensive than we could afford. But, we made an offer within our budget, and it was accepted. It was a joy to have groups in.

One thing that I always try to do at church is to greet new people visiting the church and make sure they feel welcome. This habit came in handy when I became membership chair of the United Methodist Women.

Patience

I've always felt that I had a good supply of patience in my relationships. I've always said that my church family takes the place of my family not being nearby.

And, I feel that marriage is a situation one goes into that requires a lot of work. One should always think of the needs of your partner as much or more than your own needs. In the long run, you are simply helping each other grow together in your thoughts and actions, which leads to harmony. Speaking more broadly, any relationship requires thought and consideration.

Joys of Sharing Love

Drennan and I would drive down to Stratford Harbour. It was a beautiful drive, and we didn't need to talk a lot. Just being together was a feeling of love and caring. Sometimes I would think, "Why aren't we talking?" Then I would realize that we can enjoy being together without having to talk all the time. I'm sure there were many women who would have been upset and thought something was wrong with them if their husband didn't want to be in a conversation, but it didn't bother me. I understood what his needs were.

Leaving the World a Better Place to Live

I believe that we definitely should support the organizations that are making the world a better place to live in. Public TV: Its aim and goal is to produce programs that are truly informative and educational. I've always tried to ensure that what I'm giving money to is a worthwhile cause. Another example is Society of Saint Andrew, which is trying to feed the hungry in the United States. And, by giving to Wesley Seminary to help build church leadership, the world is changed.

Enjoying Good Music

I played the violin with the symphony in high school. God has given some people the ability to create good music, sing, and play, and filled them with the desire to share it. It was my good fortune to be chairman of the music committee for several years at my church.

When the church was in need of a better instrument in the sanctuary, the opportunity arose that a Steinway "B" piano could be purchased at a special price that was too good to pass up: It would be the best instrument out there that you could buy. I wanted to give the very best instrument to the church, which was this Steinway "B" grand, "B" referring to the size. So, I had the joy of giving this special instrument to be used for music to the glory of God. Without the hands to play it, it would be of no value, but we have the hands at our church. A good instrument makes all the difference. I rationalized spending this amount of money this way: I figured 10 percent (a tithe) of what I owned belonged to God anyway, and that I should spend the money for this particular piano. I've received many, many comments of appreciation. I was giving God back what really was due Him to express my gratitude for the many blessings that I've had in my life over the years.

Super Vitamin B Complex Plus C

From a practical part of life, here is my story about Super Vitamin B Complex Plus C, which has all the B vitamins in it:

In the 1960s, when I could not go up and down steps because my right knee was weak and inflamed, my doctor prescribed aspirin to reduce the inflammation and suggested that I might take some Super Vitamin B Complex to see if it would help my knee heal. I thought to myself, "If I'm taking this to help my knee get well, why not keep on taking it to keep it well?"

About two years later I asked my doctor, who had retired, if I was doing any harm in continuing to take Super Vitamin B Complex Plus C, and she said, "No, it is water soluble, so it just washes through if the body doesn't need it."

I kept on taking it for 35 years, until about the year 2000. Since I was taking a multi-vitamin, I just stopped taking B Complex. Soon pain wracked my neck, back, and legs, and I was miserable. I asked the doctor for some pain relief, but then I remembered that I had stopped taking the Super Vitamin B Complex. I immediately put myself back on it, and before long I didn't need medicine and I was having no further pain.

Now, more than 101, I take another Super Vitamin B Complex Plus C whenever I have pain in my knees or hands. At a dosage of four tablets a day, I live pain free.

If you put yourself on Super Vitamin B Complex therapy, don't expect results in a few days. It may take a few weeks.

Coda

I have learned many, many things during these many years. Things that I wish I had known then that I know now.

All along the way I heard Mother say, "A penny saved is a penny earned, and you don't pay taxes on it."

There are only two things we have to do in life: pay taxes and die. I'm happy to pay my taxes because it gives us good places to live. And, I'm happy to die. As I approach the last years of my journey, things are going to be great. I'm going to live fully and do God's work until I get to the pearly gates. I remember the little prayer I said each night as a child: "Now I lay me down to sleep, I pray the Lord my soul to keep. If I should die before I wake, I pray the Lord my soul to take."

I hope you have enjoyed reading this book as much as I've enjoyed living life during my journey.

There is one more thought I would like to share with you: The world is in a terrible economic situation, and governments are trying to emerge from the economic recession that we're in. If people would work together today as we did back in the '40s for good schools, this would be a different world to live in. What I'm referring to is this: If members of Congress were elected to serve the people of society and were sent to Washington to work for the good of the country instead of for special interests and in getting what they can for themselves, their districts and their states, we would be living in a better country than the one we're living in now.

It was such a joy to work for the good of the community in the '40s when we were working for good schools. We came up with one of the best school systems in the country because no one was working for his or her own selfish interest. If the same philosophy were applied to the federal government, we would have a wonderful country.

Index

A

B

C

D

E

F

G

L

M

R

S

Y

Yellowstone National Park 215
Yokel, William 2, 35-36

Yugoslavia 197, 199

Z

Zajac, Susan "Sue" 234, 241
Zeus, Temple of 225

Zimmerman, Chris 242